IMMIGRATION TO TRANSTIERRO

IMMIGRATION TO TRANSTIERRO
A Bilingual, Bicultural and Bifurcated Life

KEISELIM A. MONTÁS

TRANSLATED BY
ERIN GOODMAN

escribana
books
an imprint of artepoética press

ISBN-10: 1-952336-38-4
ISBN-13: 978-1-952336-38-6

To my child, Mía, for whom I hope to be able to do as much as my mom did for me.

To my mom, Natividad Díaz, who like so many immigrant parents held a piece-wage job at a towel factory in Brooklyn and never learnt to speak English. The word Gratitude barely comes close...

CONTENTS

CONCLUSION

AFTERWORD

NOTES

BIBLIOGRAPHY

INDEX

IMMIGRATION TO TRANSTIERRO

FOREWORD

Territories of Migration: Transnationality, Hybrid Identities, and Linguistic Practices

In the collective imagination, migration often refers to the movement of indefinite masses of individuals from one territory to another, driven mostly by economic or political necessity. This highly simplified vision transforms migrants into a sort of uniform entity, in which each individual automatically loses all distinctive traits and peculiarities: the mass is labeled and categorized based on generic parameters such as birthplace or origin, language, or skin color. Yet behind these generalizing categories lie human beings, each with their own history, identity, culture, and traditions. As Ambrosini (2005: 16) emphasizes, anyone approaching the topic of migration "must first be aware of the heterogeneity and fluidity of the processes that can be labeled as migration" and of the multiple profiles of immigrants, who can be "migrants for work, seasonal or contract workers, skilled immigrants and entrepreneurs, [immigrants] for family reunification, refugees and asylum seekers, irregular immigrants, victims of trafficking, second generation migrants, return migrants, etc." (ibid., pp. 21-26). Consequently, the very definition of migration encompasses a complexity of conditions that cannot be reduced to a single, unique meaning.

For this reason, since the early 2000s, scientific studies have progressively broadened their horizons on the issue of migration by adopting an interdisciplinary approach (Foner,

2003) with the aim of also exploring the individual dimension of migration: as Suárez-Orozco noted in 2003, "the next generation of anthropological studies on immigration will increasingly be called upon to systematically engage with the approaches and findings of colleagues in related disciplines and to continue to champion the value of the unique perspectives that emerge from the ethnographic process" (p. 55). The combination of historical, sociological, anthropological, ethnographic, linguistic, geopolitical, and literary perspectives has, therefore, allowed for a qualitative investigation not only of the consequences but also of the meanings of the act of migration. In this way, the term migration has begun to lose that aura of impersonality that had perhaps long distinguished it, taking on a more specific, more intimate meaning, tied to the concrete experience of the migrant, whose existence unfolds across two poles: the country of origin and the country of arrival.

It is in this context that Keiselim A. Montás' work, IMMIGRATION TO TRANSTIERRO ("*De la emigración al transtierro*" in its original Spanish version) enriches the contemporary debate by revisiting the concept of *transtierro*, developed by Spanish philosopher José Gaos in the 1940s to describe the plight of exiles from the Spanish Civil War. Gaos used it to describe the condition of those exiled from the Spanish Civil War: a neologism formed from the prefix trans- –"beyond, across"– and the noun tierra. There is a strong assonance with two other Spanish terms with the same root: entierro, which in Italian translates as burial, and destierro, meaning exile. Both seem to somehow refer to the term transtierro. Entierro is formed from the preposition "en," which means "inside," "toward the interior," and tierra, which can therefore be literally translated as "inside the earth." The word destierro, on the other hand, is formed from the privative prefix des-, meaning "separation," "deprivation," and terra, meaning "deprived of land." These two meanings are also found in the term transtierro: because those who leave their country for other shores are called, on the one hand, to bury, forget, and leave behind everything they have built in their homeland—home, identity, culture, language, traditions, family, friendships—; on the other, they suffer deprivation, separation, or estrangement from their roots, knowledge, habits, those fixed points, in short, on which they have built their existence since birth. Thus, elaborating on the notion introduced by José Gaos, Montás uses the analytical category of transtierro to describe the experience of Caribbean migrants from Puerto Rico, the Dominican Republic, and Cuba in the United States: their living "entre tierras," suspended between two worlds, in that liminal zone that Bhabha has defined as "third space" (1994), a hybrid place where, through the encounter of different cultures, new identity configurations are formed. Montás focuses his attention precisely on this space of continuous negotiation in which the migrant is called to reconstruct his or her identity, in that in-between where they will soon no longer belong to their homeland, which will change and evolve with the passage of time, nor to their country of arrival, where they are and will forever remain a migrant.

§§§

Transtierro or In-Between

While Gaos coined the term *transtierro* to specifically refer to Spanish exiles who found refuge in México and managed to integrate into Mexican society, aided in part by linguistic factors, Montás elaborates on the concept proposed by the Spanish philosopher, indicating transtierro as the condition of fragmentation experienced by migrants forced to constantly negotiate the two opposite poles of belonging—to the abandoned country of origin—and dislocation—to the country of arrival where they are and remain foreigners. The transtierro, therefore, becomes a direct cause and a permanent condition of migration, well described by Lobera Serrano (2010: 54): "I who speak, am, now, a foreigner, a stranger, someone who arrived from outside no matter how many years ago, because I remain a foreigner even after more than 40 years, and because in the very long span of a lifetime I have transformed into someone else so many times. Today, perhaps, I almost no longer remember my people, and they too perceive me, perhaps, as a stranger." The transtierro, therefore, is that space that in English is defined as in-between, that is, in the middle, which physically does not exist but is located exactly halfway between the country of origin and the country of arrival. A suspended space, where everything remains simultaneously immobile and in move-ment: because it is formed by the memory of what the country of origin was and the urgencies of the here and now of the country of arrival, where it is necessary to rebuild and recons-truct oneself in another context, often initially alien. Two opposite poles that merge and converge in that middle ground where we end up living clothed in a social, cultural, and linguistic duplicity that undermines stability and disorientates, but with which we must inexorably reckon.

Alexander Wandl, who studied various cases of urban development in Europe to define the characteristics of those settlements, which are located halfway between metropolitan and rural areas, offered an interesting definition, "dispersed," to physically indicate the lands in-between: "The choice of the term 'territory' in territories-in-between was made to underline the relational nature of dispersed urban areas, the result of systems of relations. These sometimes interact with each other and sometimes operate in complete ignorance of each other. On the other hand, a territory cannot be conceived without borders or without control over geographical spaces. This means that it allows us to locate, map, and understand the interaction of different systems within given boundaries. Furthermore, it allows us to identify, plan, and design them on the basis of physical structures, as a territory and even as an artefact of past interactions of relational systems" (Wandl, 2014: 25). Although, as an urban planner, he referred concretely and materially to these intermediate areas, the definition proposed by Wandl is also useful for understanding what the "immaterial" in-between of the migrant means: a third space constructed through systems of relationships between two (or more) places (country of origin and country of arrival), which can be considered as a "historical artefact" as it is also the result of previous interactions.

§§§

Migration, Transnational Identities, and Networks

In reality, migrants are called upon to engage with multiple systems of relationships, which are not exclusively based on the two countries of origin and destination, but involve a wide variety of social, linguistic, and cultural models that coexist in the space between these two poles. Consequently, these models lead to the development of fluid and complex identities that migrants tend to adopt in relation to the different contexts they encounter. "Within their complex network of social relationships, transmigrants draw on fluid and multiple identities, rooted simultaneously in their societies of origin and their host societies. While some migrants identify more strongly with one society than the other, the majority appear to maintain multiple identities that simultaneously connect them to more than one nation" (Schiller, Basch, Blanc-Szanton, 1992: 11). These are transnational identities (Vertovec, 2009) developed by diasporic communities (Appadurai, 1996) who, in addition to interacting with communities present in the host country, also maintain contact with the country of origin (Calvi, 2018), thus generating the system of relationships that forms the basis of the processes of reterritorialization and identity negotiation of which they become, at the same time, the main actors and recipients. In this way, at the analytical level, "new interpretative scenarios open up which, [...] abandoning 'bipolar' models representing the migrant as an 'uprooted' person struggling to 'assimilate' into the immigration context, [allow] us to account for the presence and action of migrant groups 'simultaneously' in different places" (Riccio, 2014: 12). This is because, as Mariottini (2012: 120) points out, the individual simultaneously belongs to "different networks and the connections between network members develop in various directions, going beyond its own boundaries", where networks are understood as arbitrary and flexible relationships as specified by Barnes (1954: 43): "Every person is, so to speak, in contact with a certain number of other people, some of whom are in direct contact with each other and others are not. Likewise, everyone has a certain number of friends, who in turn have their own friends; some of a person's friends know each other, others do not. I find it convenient to define a social field of this type as a network. The resulting image is that of a set of points, some of which are connected by lines. The points represent people, or sometimes groups, while the lines indicate which people interact with each other."

§§§

Language as a Tool for (Re)constructing Identity

Within these contexts of *"superdiversity"* (Vertovec, 2007: 1), a concept used to define "a form of complexity that [...] is charac-terized by the dynamic intertwining of variables linked to a growing number of new, small, and dispersed immigrants of multiple origins, transnationally connected, socioeconomically diverse, and legally stratified, who have arrived in the last decade," the cultural and linguistic identities of migrants develop through social processes that occur in specific contexts of interaction. Identity, in fact, "is not something that speakers 'own,' but something that emerges through interactional practices—including the ways in which language is used—in contexts. Since identity is continuously and consistently produced and reproduced, delineated and shaped, and often coconstructed by the 'self' and the 'other,' we must strive to show how identities are (re)produced through language (and other media) and how they take shape through social inter-action" (De Fina, Schiffrin, Bamberg, 2006: 22). Language, therefore, "in addition to being an instrument of thought and a cultural object, is a cognitive organizer of experiential data, a means of establishing social relationships, a vehicle of rational and affective experiences, of feelings, thoughts, and emo-tions" (Mariottini, 2012: 137), which is used as a tool for creating interactions in multiethnic and multicultural spaces, within which daily encounters between different histories, languages, and cultures are reproduced. And it is through socialization that identity is renegotiated in a discursive way, precisely through language, which constitutes "a dynamic entity that adapts to the context and in turn reshapes it" (Calvi, 2014: 9).

§§§

Spaces of Identity and Linguistic Negotiation: The Linguistic Landscape

For at least two decades, scientific research in Italy [for exam-ple] has also begun to focus more deeply on these spaces of social, cultural, linguistic, and identity negotiation, especially in relation to the manifestations of languages in public spaces. This research follows the line of research pioneered by Landry and Bourhis, who, in 1997, coined the term "Linguistic Landscape" (LL) to indicate the "language of public road signs, billboards, street names, place names, shop signs, and public signs on government buildings," which "can perform two fundamental functions: one informative and one symbolic" (Landry and Bourhis, 1997: 25). Indeed, observing LL provides useful information for "interpreting the stratification of social changes and their semiotic and linguistic manifestations, as well as the values and ideologies attributed to languages" (Calvi, 2018: 9), and, with regard to the LL of migration, it constitutes an indicator that reflects the processes by which migrants "on the one hand, reaffirm their sense of belonging to their culture of origin and, on the other, mark their presence in the host society in a continuous construction of identity" (Ariolfo, 2019: 630). Consequently, by adopting an interdisciplinary approach, it was also possible to delve deeper into the relationship between language, territory, and the identity of migrant communities, as LL reflects the status of languages and the groups of speakers who use them, including identities, ideologies, and power dynamics.

The coexistence of multiple linguistic communities in large metropolises, understood as the group of people who speak a given language or linguistic variety and share its norms of use, leads to the occurrence of social and discursive practices that take shape within urban spaces, which, consequently, become theatres of continuous socio-cultural and linguistic processes: and it is in these contexts that phenomena such as code switching, that is, the passage from one linguistic variety to another during a single communicative episode, or translanguaging, the mode of negotiation of meaning used by bilinguals in a context of superdiversity (García, Wei, 2014), are recorded, which can depend on various factors, such as the social role of the interlocutor, the topic being discussed, the communicative situation, etc. Observing the communicative practices of diasporic communities, therefore, allows us to gain important insights into the perception of language as a factor of identity and a uniting force, because "the use of one's own language in social communication demonstrates, on the one hand, a positive attitude toward one's cultural origins, and on the other, the group's desire to make itself visible in the space in which it operates. In this sense, the visibility of a language influences and strengthens social bonds within the community that shares its norms and, at the same time, determines the attitudes and behaviors of other sociolinguistic groups" (Mariottini, 2019a: 628).

This means that urban space, understood in its social and cultural configuration as a historical and symbolic product, and in its subjective dimension as individual perception and experience (Krefeld, 2002), is no longer considered from a neutral perspective, but as someone's space, that is, from the perspective of those who live in it, perceive it, travel through it, operate in it, and speak it (Tani, 2018). In this way, the perspective of speakers and their perception of linguistic space has become the object of research, in what has been defined as linguistic folk, which focuses on the complexity of linguistic space through the linguistic practices and attitudes of speakers who redraw social, political, geographical, and cultural boundaries through new forms of contact that profoundly undermine the more traditional representation of space, languages, and cultures as homogeneous wholes. Linguistic space, therefore, ceases to be an abstract entity, but presents itself as a dynamic construction shaped by the communicative practices and subjective perceptions of speakers, which make it continually the object of identity and cultural redefinition.

In Italy [for example], within this context, an important line of research is dedicated to the presence, visibility, and vitality of the Spanish language in the country, especially in relation to the discursive practices of resident Hispanic-American communities. Such studies have begun to proliferate in tandem with the growth of the Spanish-speaking population in the country: according to ISTAT data, between 2019 and 2023, there was an increase of approximately 20,000 Hispanic-American migrants in Italy, with Milan the leading destination city (73,057 residents), Rome second (36,152), and Genoa third (18,415). For research on the presence and visibility of American varieties of Spanish in Italy, I would point to the works of Calvi and Uberti Bona on Milan, Mariottini and Oricchio on Rome, and Ariolfo on Genoa.

§§§

Conclusion

In this volume, Montás focuses particularly on the linguistic question, precisely because language is considered a fundamental tool in the migratory experience, both from an identity-building and symbolic perspective. The condition of bilingualism and biculturality thus becomes a paradigm of a subjectivity in constant transition, and the oscillation between the mother tongue and that of the host country becomes a metaphor for the condition of the migrant, forced to manage the constant tension between loss and recovery, assimilation and resistance, shedding light on the different ways in which migrants confront the experience of dislocation and the language barrier. "People, in fact, inhabit a multilingual world and constantly slip from culture to culture: the shift from one linguistic context to another is accompanied by a movement, from one vision of the world to another, to a new way of interpreting the circumstances of everyday life and of percei-ving oneself in relation to the social groups that compose it" (Mariottini, 2013: 492).

The Dominican author, in addition to enriching the text

with a reconstruction of the historical trajectories of migration from the Spanish-speaking Caribbean to the United States, which began in the early 1900s, also delves into the transnational political and economic processes that accompanied Caribbean migration to the United States. He invites us to understand the concept of transtierro not only as a marginal or temporary experience, but as a paradigmatic condition of contemporary migration, which reflects the difficulties of integration and, at the same time, the need to reconstruct new, hybrid, and transnational identities, including linguistic ones.

And this is precisely where the originality of Montás' contribution lies: in restoring voice and human depth to an experience too often reduced to statistical categories or media stereotypes. The transtierro emerges as both a theoretical lens and an existential testimony, capable of demonstrating how the migrant is not a body in transit but a subject in relation, an individual who inhabits the space of in-between, transforming it into a laboratory of cultural and linguistic creativity. This book, therefore, is not only about Caribbean migrants in the United States, but also speaks to each of us, reminding us that migration is one of the foundational experiences of contemporary life, an indispensable key to understanding the identity, political, and linguistic dynamics of our time.

ALESSANDRO ORICCHIO
Sapienza University of Rome

IMMIGRATION TO TRANSTIERRO

INTRODUCTION

This book was born out of a need to explain to an academic audience how it is possible to exist as a creative, bilingual, bicultural being, who has to navigate between two worlds on a daily basis. The project originated with a look in the mirror, a self-examination, a self-explanation that was followed by a look around me, at my environment and my contemporaries, and at my history and the history of those who share similar circumstances.

From this explanation I have come to define "TRANS-TIERRO" as the present life condition of people who emigrated from their countries and live or survive as immigrants in another country with a different culture, system, language, and customs, while maintaining a real or imaginary connection with their countries of origin. Although the context of this book is limited to origin countries in the Spanish-speaking Caribbean islands (Cuba, Puerto Rico, and the Dominican Republic), and to the United States as the host country and backdrop of the transtierro, I am open to the possibility that this condition, and the circumstances that lead to it, are applicable to similar migratory circumstances from the rest of Latin America and many other parts of the world to the United States, or similar circumstances in any part of the world where emigration and settlement occur from a developing country to a developed country with a different culture, system, language, and customs. I would offer that the emotional transtierro (not so much the practical and economic ones) plays out in the same way, regardless of the to and from, of any immigration experience.

§§§

To develop the idea of this existence as transtierro, in the first chapter I begin by presenting the term in its historical context, and then by redefining it and differentiating it from its previous definitions and applications. I then go on to define and contrast the term with the concept of exile and clarify that although the migratory motives for exile may vary, when it occurs over a long period of time—as is the case with Cuban exile—it evolves into the condition of transtierro. This book's first publication came out just as the normalization of relations between Cuba and the United States was announced (in December 2014), and though it was still too early to be sure, I surmised that once diplomatic normalization took effect and political impediments were eliminated, Cuban exiles would not return en masse to Cuba, and that their condition would go from exiles to trans-terrados.

I present a series of particulars to describe the immigrant landscape in the new country, and I observe a number of factors that play a determining role in the trajectory and establishment of the newcomer. Using this framework, I examine determinants such as education level, socioeconomic class, age, reasons for emigrating, occupation, place of arrival, etc. Based on these factors, I define and exemplify the resulting potential identities immigrants can adopt, using the language in which individuals communicate as a touchstone and identity portal. I outline the alternatives or strategies of *Assimilation* (taking on the OTHER identity), *Rejection* (attachment to a SINGULAR identity), and a *Bilingual Alternative* (coexistence of both identities), that occur as a solution or resolution to the conflicts of identity and survival that we are exposed to through the experience of emigration.

§ § §

In the second chapter, I proceed to present a historical summary of Caribbean emigration in the context of the diplomatic or political relations of each of the three countries with the United States, pausing to comment on the major migratory waves and the numbers of people who emigrated at various important periods. This summary is interwoven with the factors presented in the first chapter and I include figures who are representative of transtierro in the case of each country. These people, through their linguistic identity and literary production, serve as evidence of my theory on the condition of TRANSTIERRO. But beyond listing certain key figures, I present their qualities and testimonies, which serve to support the proposed considerations and demonstrate that we do in fact live in a condition of permeability between two cultures. In essence, a bilingual, bicultural, and bifurcated life.

§ § §

The third chapter is like a parenthesis to address the issue of diaspora. This should be self-evident: we are diaspora. Yet it remains a questionable subject in certain intellectual circles. By introducing this issue, I attempt to establish the point as a given; and, in a concise manner, I posit that the term is equally applicable to a single person as it is to an entire community.

§ § §

The fourth and final chapter focuses on the realm of my personal experience as a transterrado. Here, and beginning with my condition as a creative being that has always had a close relationship with language, I explore the factors that make up transtierro on a personal level, establishing the context of introduction to the new language within the framework of my relationship with writing as a creative outlet. From there I go on to address the aspects of the *Bilingual Alternative* — linguistic hybridity, the duality of living in two languages and between two cultures, swearing loyalty to two countries. I also discuss my creative practice, how translation represents a vehicle for being understood in both languages, and finally, how this condition manifests in terms of my identity.

Estaciones

Un claro de bosque, aquí
a horas tempranas de la mañana
        a la caída de la tarde allá
una primavera finalmente resuelta, como un telón
de escenografía de pronto desplegado
       un verano maduro, cuajado
      de arándanos jugosos y moras de la tierra
un riachuelo bordeado de helechos nuevos
y súbitas flores silvestres
     una hierba gramínea de espigas inclinadas y rubias
      como crines de bosque cargadas de cigarras
pinos
de múltiples y largos brazos desperezados
      de múltiples y torpes brazos agotados
como vencidos de sí mismos, del invierno que se ha
   ido
       del invierno que se viene.

RAÚL BUENO
Misivas de la Nueva Albión
(Cascahuesos Editores, 2014)

Seasons

A clearing in the forest, here
In the early morning hours

At the afternoon's arrival there

a spring finally realized, as a theatre's
curtains swiftly raised

a ripe summer, full
of juicy blueberries and berries of the earth

a brook edging the sprouting ferns
and wildflowers suddenly sprung

a grassy herb of long bowed sprigs and blond as manes
of woodlands full of cicadas

pine trees
of multiple and long stretched out arms

of multiple and clumsy exhausted arms

like neighbors of each other, of the winter that just
      left

of the winter that is coming.

RAÚL BUENO
Misivas de la Nueva Albión
(poem translation into English by Keiselim A. Montás)

CHAPTER 1

TRANSTIERRO

Let us begin by introducing the term TRANSTIERRO in its historical context, and then define the current condition in which those of us, who have left our homelands to emigrate overseas in search of a better future, live and survive. The term was first introduced in the intellectual sphere in 1943, by the Spanish philosopher and exile José Gaos (1900–1969). Gaos used the term explicitly and specifically to refer to Spanish exiles in México, to show that the experience for Spaniards in México was different from that of exiles from other European countries at the time. By 'transtierro,' Gaos meant that the Spaniards encountered a certain linguistic and cultural continuity, which allowed them to continue and expand the political-cultural endeavors they had undertaken in Spain. He also emphasized that given the generous welcome from the Mexican government and people, México became "the 'extension' and 'destination' of the homeland itself, to be called 'empatriates.' That is, 'empa-triates' are understood not as having left their homeland for a foreign one, but rather as having transferred from one home-land to another. This extension and destination distances the term from what is understood by 'desterrado,' to be specified as transterrado."[1] In this context, 'transterrado' can be understood as the continuation of what is Spanish in México. Here is an analogy to illustrate the meaning of the term according to Gaos: If transterrado were applied to a plant that is brought from

Spain and planted in México, such as a Valencian orange tree, then it is transplanted. In México it continues to produce Valencian oranges, as the climate is just as favorable for orange trees.

I will use the term TRANSTIERRO (and 'transterrado') here with a new meaning that moves away from the idea of continuity proposed by Gaos. In order to define this condition of our existence, I affirm and highlight our transitory circums-tances, or circumstances of transit, as well as rupture. The Spanish-speaking Caribbean island countries emigrant who arrives in the United States is faced with a different landscape, both geographically and culturally: another language, other customs, and, in most cases, another climate. A transition from Toledo to Guadalajara is not the same as a transition from Santiago de los Caballeros to Chicago.

Focusing on that transitory circumstance, which connects the extremes of rupture–continuity like a hyphen, I will refer to the term transtierro in its applicability to those of us who live on that bridge that connects us with our multiple realities and identities, on the one hand—the reality of the world in which we live and survive, *vis à vis* the reality of that other world we came from and with which we keep in touch. And on the other hand, the identity with which we interact in our daily lives (including our workplaces, the people we spend time with, and in what language we communicate during our lunch hour, etc.), *vis à vis* the identity we embody at home and with which we interact with family and friends both in the new country and in the country of origin.

This transtierro could be illustrated as *trans – tierro* or 'between lands' if we contextualize it in parallel with the word transatlantic: on the other side or across the Atlantic. That is, not on one side or the other, but in the middle, on the imaginary bridge, in the intermediate space that connects the two sides of that ocean. Here the prefix 'trans-' (in both meanings of "to the other side" and "through") must be taken literally as a physical place or space. If we mentally place ourselves in the meaning of "on the other side," we realize that it positions us physically or mentally on one end or side of something, but with our gaze and intention fixed or pointing towards the other end or side. Likewise, if we place ourselves in the meaning of "through," the resulting physical or mental position is in the middle, neither on one side or the other. On the basis of this position, we can posit that transtierro is *the condition that defines those of us who are (physically, mentally, or emotionally) between lands, countries, homelands, homes, etc.—those of us who are not entirely on one side or the other.* It is worth noting that today this is a universal condition as a direct result of emigration, which is what humans have done throughout history in order to survive.

If we accept the term as an intermediate space, then we can easily see how the analogy of the transplanted orange tree is complicated if applied to the new reality/condition. A Valencian orange tree cannot be planted and immediately continue to produce oranges in Chicago or Portland; this would require a currently non-existent process of grafting or genetic adaptation. Such an experiment would depend on whether a tree (i.e. the person) is brought in and placed in an area with a certain amount of climatization—for instance, a neighborhood like Washington Heights in Manhattan, or Little Havana in Miami—which would be the best but slowest transition for adult migrants; or whether a bud is brought and grafted onto a tree trunk with the genetic disposition to stay alive in winter (as in the case of child arrivals); or whether the tree is brought in and the trunk is cut and (if the roots survive) a genetically altered fruit bud is grafted onto it, whose output would not necessarily be a Valencian orange but could even become something else—an apple or a peach (which would be the extreme case of a painful transformation that I will address later).

Today there are millions of people who have left their homelands in search of a better life; they have done so to a certain extent willingly, even when they have been forced by economic or other pressures (deemed "economic exile"). In other words, they have been wishing or even aspiring to emi-grate, whether legally or illegally. Those who have immi-grated legally or have obtained legal immigration status in the United States[2] are able to return to their homeland at any time and at the slightest tinge of nostalgia maldita ("that darn nostalgia"). It is imperative to point out this transportation advantage, which today allows an emigrant from the Southern Cone, living in, let's say, New York City, to be back in their native country in a matter of fourteen hours, or an emigrant from the Caribbean to return in a matter of three or four hours. This was not so easy eighty or ninety years ago, when international travel was mostly done by ship and a bout of nostalgia did not merit a trip from México to Spain or from New York to Puerto Rico. There-fore, to a certain extent, we are talking about a condition of today's world, which through its modernity and techno-logical advances has shrunk the globe into a very small sphere, compared to the world of seven or eight decades ago. This modernity and these technological advances are what make it possible for us to stay in constant contact with what, in times past, simply and necessarily had to be left behind. Today's immigrant, unlike the immigrants of the first eight decades of the 20th century, can keep in daily contact with "their past" through television, the telephone, e-mail, social media, etc. In short, they have access to everything from newspapers to video conferences with family and friends. They remain connected, without any meaningful interruption.

§§§

EXILE

At this point, we should specify the difference between the

condition of transtierro and the traditional concept of "exile"—the circumstance of forced expatriation for political reasons. Political exile is not the result of a choice nor is it necessarily a desired condition, unlike those who have migrated voluntarily and willingly in search of a better life. On the contrary, in most cases, exile is a forced, painful, and heartbreaking condition wherein one's survival (in the worst case) and freedom (in the best) depend on leaving. Exile occurs in situations in which the individual is inevitably committed to a struggle or cause in their homeland—a fight to which they have dedicated words, saliva, sweat, blood, and life. And in an instant that individual is abruptly removed, expelled, exiled, or forced to flee, desperately and without prior notice, leaving behind everything in the past and yet to come (family, life, and property) and thus creating a circumstance of uprooting, dispossession, and death.

Exile also carries with it certain elements of guilt in relation to people left behind. Exiles may experience a kind of martyrdom and mortification, hounded by the feeling of survivor's guilt, because they cannot avoid having a heavy conscience for being alive, knowing that their comrades and relatives were left behind and exposed to dangers such as being disappeared, tortured, imprisoned, persecuted, or fleeing in order to survive. Hence the life of the exile becomes an obsessive struggle for the country (homeland) from which they have been torn.

This exile, and the concern for the situation left behind, is manifest in communications and activities, be it filing complaints, writing articles, organizing support groups, starting awareness campaigns, raising funds, etc. This also implies that for a long and indeterminate amount of time—which can last from a few months or years, to decades or a lifetime—the exile may not "unpack" at all. They will always have that suitcase ready under the bed or behind the door for when the time comes to return, because their main goal is to go back to their country, life revolves around it. There are countless stories told by the children of exiles about that feeling of living in a transitory space, where at any moment they expected their parents to tell them: "We're going back today!" It is worth citing Richard Blanco, the Cuban-American inaugural poet at Barack Obama's second presidential inauguration, who recalled that as a child he watched his father, newspaper in hand, talk with the neighbors about how things were going with the resistance in Cuba, and how Blanco thought that at any moment his father would cut the conversation short and pronounce: "We're going back to Cuba today!"

Depending on how long the stay is, exile can turn into a condition similar to transtierro or transtierro itself. This is precisely the case of the Spanish exiles in México. In 1975, General Francisco Franco died and the political conditions that had determined their exile no longer held. Then what? Gather everything, rise up, and return to the Motherland? Well, no, not necessarily; it is not so easy after so many years. Here I quote what the Spanish-Mexican philosopher, writer, and teacher Adolfo Sánchez Vázquez[3] said about the poems he wrote in México at the beginning of his exile there in the early 1940s:

> [They were] written in the hardest years, [I was] nostalgic and at the same time excited about exile in México, an exile experienced—despite the generous reception by the Mexican government and people—as the most painful loss of homeland, with the constant and hopeful obsession of an unfulfilled homecoming and, when that could [finally] be accomplished, exile had already be-come, for the survivors, 'transtierro' (*La Jornada* news-paper, 2005).

Although Adolfo Sánchez Vázquez did return to Spain, where he also taught, received various honors, and was declared an "adopted son" of Málaga, he ended up working, teaching, writing, and living the rest of his life in México, where he died at the age of 95.

In late 2014, we faced a hot-button situation when an attempt at a normalization of U.S.-Cuba relations was made by Presidents Barack Obama and Raúl Castro. It seemed inevitable that circumstances on the island would change and that the political conditions or impediments that caused exile would disappear. When that happens, the two million Cuban exiles will likely become transterrados, just like the Spaniards in México, since the roots they have put down outside of Cuba are very difficult or impossible to unearth.

The nightmare that followed, between 2016 and 2020, almost destroyed that possibility by the reversal of all diplomatic policies and posture advanced during the Obama years. While the Obama administration did abolish the "wet foot-dry foot policy," the next administration's policies and anti-immigrant rhetoric did tremendous damage to immigrant communities in the United States, and to diplomatic relations and the welcoming and democratic reputation of the United States of America (the nation's international image, its very global high ground and moral authority).

One element that helps both exiles and transterrados plant roots and develop affection for the host country, is that the host country has its own attractions, its own charms and certain advantages that the country of origin does not have to offer (which is undoubtedly the case of the United States as a host country). The United States had always offered a "warm welcome,"[4] a certain order, structure, and freedom; as well as a host of opportunities and guarantees. All of this eventually grows inside each individual and, little by little, allows them to unpack that suitcase that was always ready by the door. It is by unpacking that suitcase that the individual can truly begin to accept what the host country has to offer. And more importantly, by unpacking baggage, the individual can begin to invest and contribute civically and emotionally to the host country. This contribution is like a way of giving back or giving a little of oneself, either in reciprocity or in gratitude for what has been received from the new homeland (Stolowicz 2011, 1).

Now, whether exile is a cause and condition, or transtierro is an effect and decision, this initial displacement always
represents, emotionally and practically, countless ruptures,
losses, confusion, pain, uprooting, and nostalgia. And in the
psyche and interior, an amalgam of shared or often reinvented
identities.

§ § §

IMMIGRATION FACTORS

To fully understand the phenomenon and condition of transtierro, let us discuss what happens when a person leaves their
homeland and emigrates, either voluntarily or involuntarily, to
start over or make a new life in another country. As I indicated
earlier, I want to focus the attention on emigration from the
Spanish-speaking island countries of the Caribbean (Cuba, the
Dominican Republic, and Puerto Rico) to the United States, thus
establishing part of the framework within which I will build the
foundation of this book. However, we cannot rule out by
omission the universal experience of immigrants who come
from any other country with a different culture and language.
The traits, experiences, conditions, and experiences undoubtedly present similar effects, whether the emigration is from
Chile to Canada, from Angola to Germany, from China to Cali-
fornia, etc.

When a person first arrives in a country that represents,
in the short and long terms, a new culture and a new language,
many factors influence the adaptation process. Among such
factors, it is indispensable to denote the following:

Level of Education

The person's *level of education* is of paramount importance, because the higher the education level, the greater the potential knowledge of the culture (and in certain cases even language) of the host country and the country of origin, and therefore the faster the transition or adaptation. This can make it faster or easier to adapt but is not a guarantee in and of itself. In this educational realm, it has been proven that being illiterate in one's own language is one of the greatest obstacles faced by adult immigrants in learning the new language and navigating the new system.

Class or Socio-economic Status

Although there is generally a direct correlation between *socio-economic status* and education level, this is not always the case, particularly in the Caribbean where, due to a lack of institutionalism, as is the case of the Dominican Republic, a person may have a low or non-existent education level and still belong to the high echelons of power or attain a high socio-economic level. And on the other hand, given a certain abundance of institutionalism, such as in Cuba, a person can have a high level of education and belong to a low socio-economic level. I have cited Cuba and the Dominican Republic as extreme cases, where a surgeon makes a living as a waiter, or today's waiter could be a senator, governor or ambassador, or a millionaire tomorrow. Taking these caveats into account, coming from a high socio-economic position generally eases the newcomer's transition in terms of the practical aspects of daily life (residence, food, school) and allows for greater access to the country of origin (either from more frequent phone calls, or from regular trips and visits).

Age at Time of Emigration

The *person's age* is practically proportional to their ability to absorb the new culture and language: the younger the person, the easier it is. This, however, can be complicated, as it will more palpably bring them closer to a linguistic duality that over time will make it difficult for them to reintegrate into the culture of the "motherland," and it will not guarantee their complete immersion in the new culture and language. In a short time, young immigrants become the first to inhabit that bridge on which the transterrado lives and survives, since they inevitably and immediately enter the duality of two (sometimes contradictory) worlds: their parents' world and the one they face outside the doors of the home. Therefore, they are forced to constantly negotiate both worlds in a permeable way. The influence of age can be divided into at least three stages: 1) *childhood arrivals*; 2) *the literate* (those who arrive young, had begun their education in the home country and are already literate); and 3) *adults* who arrive at least of working age, with or without prior education.

1) Childhood Arrivals: Those who arrive in their infancy or childhood, depending on their upbringing and their parents' options and choices, will be the second category to whom the term or condition of transterrado is applicable, since they will become aware of their condition as they are integrated into civil society. They are generally educated and become literate in a single language, they grow up with the need to use that one language to talk with teachers and friends, to develop their social relationships and to interact with their present and surrounding world. And they use another language to communicate with parents and relatives, which is like maintaining or establishing ties with their parents' 'other world,' which little by little will become foreign to them. In the United States, these children grow up with the English language on the tip of their tongues and "American culture" all around them, and with the language and culture of their parents in their ears, heart, blood, skin color, and hair. They have a certain pride for (and identification with) the left-behind homeland in their subconscious, although at the same time that homeland seems more and more like a kind of fairy tale or fantasy world where everything is different. Meanwhile, that homeland left behind does not know them, and will never recognize them. They are the first who unknowingly must swear allegiance to two cultures and two countries, neither of which will ever fully accept them.

Consider the case of Pulitzer Prize winner Junot Díaz, author of *Drown*, *The Brief Wondrous Life of Oscar Wao*, and *This Is How You Lose Her*. In the United States he is considered a "Dominican-American" writer, and in the Dominican Republic there are those who staunchly refuse to recognize him as a Dominican. This is a subject of constant debate. (It is worth noting that no one calls William Carlos Williams an American-Puerto Rican poet, even though his mother was Puerto Rican.) Díaz represents the perfect paradigm: his life is like an embodiment of this condition, while his work bears witness to this adaptation process. It is not unreasonable to theorize that Díaz's work is so popular (and so well-received) because it reflects the stories and processes of immigrants from all over the world. It is true that there are other writers who have addressed the issue of transition, such as Cuban-American writer Cristina García (*Dreaming in Cuban*), Dominican-American writer Julia Álvarez (*How the García Girls Lost Their Accent*), and Puerto Rican writer Piri Thomas (*Down These Mean Streets*), to name a few. But Junot Díaz has managed to unfold and extend beyond the contours of the aforementioned *Latinidad*, arriving at a time when those of his condition and generation (with a shared experience) have access to this story in unprecedented ways.

2) The Literate: Those who emigrate as young people, literate in the native language and having completed a certain level of education, confront the new language face to face upon entering school, and thus acquire their linguistic skills in an accelerated way, driven by a need for survival. They are the first to whom the term or condition of 'transterrados' applies, since they immediately become their parents' assistants, helping them navigate the new system, culture, and language on a daily basis. They are the interpreters at medical appointments, in stores, banks, government offices, and schools. They are immediately obliged to jump on the transterrado bridge, forced to imme-diately navigate, as hybrids, between the new culture, language, and system in which their parents now need to make a living, and the old language, system and culture in which their parents still operate. They have the opportunity or advantage of growing up bilingual and bicultural.

3) Adults: Adults who arrive of working age, particularly of low or middle educational and socio-economic levels (as is the majority), inevitably suffer the most and statistically end up as monolingual transterrados. Nonetheless, they immediately recognize the advantages and opportunities offered by the new country and the new culture. They are the ones who end up harboring that hope of one day returning to their homeland, of one day going back to being the individuals they once were. Therefore, it will take them much longer to adopt this new condition of transterrados, consciously or unconsciously. When illiterate adults arrive, language adjustment becomes almost impossible. Lacking an educational base in their mother tongue, they cannot make the transition. The void is not only linguistic: in many cases there is a cultural and knowledge gap in the broadest sense.

Reasons for Emigrating

The *reasons for emigrating* play a large role in terms of how strong or weak the connection is with the country of origin, and how frequent the contact is. We have pointed out that when the reason is exile, the connection is much stronger or as strong as the experience of uprooting. Beyond exile, the motivations for emigrating can be as trivial as a whim for adventure or to flex wealth, but in the majority of cases people are motivated by economic necessity. Therefore, emigrants, for reasons of economic improvement, live an existential duality: on the one hand, they want to bring over their family and, on the other, they dream of a definitive return. That is, a homecoming to their native country with accumulated assets to start a business and live peacefully and prosperously for the rest of their days (much like in a fairy tale). Many immigrants make this desire a reality, but they later return to the United States when they realize that their country of origin does not have and cannot offer the infrastructural guarantees to sustain the established businesses, or because they already have left behind children, belongings, and roots in the host country.

Attitude Towards the New Country

The *attitude towards the new country* is a determining factor in relation to how long it will take for the individual to begin to unpack their suitcase: to accept, recognize, integrate, and begin to contribute to the host country. This attitude is closely linked to the political-historical situation of the country of origin and its relationship with the host country. The attitude of a Cuban exile towards the United States may be very different from that of a Nicaraguan or Dominican or Puerto Rican refugee or exile, since the historical framework of the United States' relationship with these countries has very marked tonalities and differentiations: sometimes the U.S. is seen as an ally and other times as an invader. When the attitude tends toward the vision of the host country as an imperialist invader, immigrants will constantly resist accepting the benefits of the host country and will show little interest in integrating into its civic and political life. However, visits to the homeland offer a glimpse of the contrast and, little by little, not only does acceptance begin to manifest itself in practice, but even the rhetoric tends to abate.

Job or Occupation

The newcomer's *job or occupation* is a factor that is often ignored but plays a decisive role in their adaptation to new environments. The best-case scenario is when the individual can practice the same profession or occupation they did in their country of origin, which allows them a certain stability, balance, sense of self-worth and security in an environment that easily lends itself to the newcomer feeling incapable, useless, and inept. It will also be of influence who their co-workers are, who can serve as supportive guides as they navigate the new system and practical and socio-cultural differences. Of course, there is always the chance that some co-worker will be a constant annoyance for the newcomer—scoffing at every mistake or fumble; this sometimes will serve as a stimulus to improve and other times it will be like an anchor that ties them to the depths of their situation.

The New Place

The *place* where the newcomer comes to live—their city, town, or neighborhood—will perhaps be one of the factors with the greatest influence on their development and adaptation. Locations can represent advantages and disadvantages from multiple perspectives. A Dominican who arrives in Washington Heights will find it much easier to navigate those first months or years in the new country, compared, for example, to someone who arrives in Des Moines, Iowa. However, in a matter of four or five years (having survived the most difficult first few years), the one who arrived in Washington Heights will continue to eat plantains and, if then they had to move to a city like Des Moines, they would be forced to start over in a new culture and language, almost like if arriving for the first time. On the other hand, a person who arrives straight to Des Moines (and survives those first years there) will crave *mangú de plátano* and yearn for their homeland. They will feel more Dominican than the *tambora* and, if forced to relocate to any other city in the

United States (including a neighborhood like Washington Heights), they could do so with much less difficulty and suffering.

Arriving in a neighborhood of compatriots can represent a trap for adult immigrants belonging to intellectual or literary circles, since they can very easily isolate themselves within the host country and establish an intellectual and creative life strictly circumscribed to the old world. In this way, they never fully explore the cultural attractions that the host country offers —from academic centers and large libraries and bookstores to museums, galleries, cultural centers, and so on. In many cases, they never become participants in the artistic, intellectual, and cultural life that takes place beyond the few blocks of their neighborhoods.

Plans for the Future

The newcomer's *plans for the future*, whether concrete plans or wishes, are of great weight and influence in terms of unpacking the suitcase and in the integration into the civic life of the new country. If the plan is to return to the country of origin as soon as possible, this will create a very difficult barrier to overcome and will be a constant impediment to take full advantage of the opportunities offered by the new homeland. If the return plan is longer-term, there are more opportunities to put down roots in the new soil. Of course, when the plan is to "stay for good," this can sow the seeds of a total break with the past, which in some cases leads to a denial of the original identity and a forced transformation (a topic that I will address when talking about the *Rejection* strategy), which does not lead to the condition of transtierro.

Distance and Connections

Lastly, let us factor in distance. *Distance and connections* with the homeland are the final factor—how far the homeland is and what ties exist to that nation. The proximity of the origin country and the ease of return are essential to facilitate constant connection and the ability to return at any moment prompted by the slightest tinge of "Nostalgia Maldita." Distance from the homeland and ease of return must be distinguished from each other: Cuba is closer to the United States than the Dominican Republic, but it is much easier to travel to the Dominican Republic than to Cuba.

The connections and ties that unite the newcomer with their homeland, whether of a political or family nature, also are very influential when it comes to continuing to plant and develop roots in the homeland. Maintaining this connection is like a necessary prerequisite or precondition for the individual to feel that they have an obligation or oath of loyalty with the culture and the homeland left behind, and by necessity they must fluctuate between the two countries, thus adapting to the condition of transtierro. The connections are usually family-based—a spouse or children left behind. These are the strongest ties that bind and connect the newcomer with the former country, through daily life and sending remittances, and in the plans of someday bringing the family to live in the "wonderful" new country (although this idea contradicts that other desire —consciously or unconsciously—to someday return to live in the origin country).

§§§

LANGUAGE OPTIONS

Recently arrived immigrants inevitably must face the new language in order to survive—not only in practice, but also to satisfy the existential need for identity, which is inextricably linked to language. Through the lens of possible linguistic alternatives, and taking into account the factors outlined above, let us delve into the experience of someone who arrives for the first time in a country with a different culture, system, and language. Firstly, all emigration represents, in and of itself, and in particular this type of emigration, an uprooting and rupture that will inevitably lead to conflicts and difficulties: this is not a vacation, rather an entirely new life. Upon arrival in the new country, the emigrant immediately goes from being a complete person with a defined identity in a familiar environment that recognizes and accepts them as part of it, to a state or situation where nothing or no one is familiar to them—not even themself. Suddenly they are in a place where they are unknown, not recognized, where their identity disappears, where the fact of their arrival turns them into an almost invisible being, without voice or vote. In short, in a matter of hours or days, the person goes from a place where they are admired or respected, or at least tolerated and accepted as part of the fabric that makes up that society—where they lived and where their parents and grandparents probably live or lived, and where the bones of their ancestors probably are buried—to doubting their own existence. In other words, suddenly they find themself in a place where their presence does not matter, where they only truly belong in the space where they are standing, in the clothes they are wearing. Absolutely nothing else is certain and every-thing could disappear at any moment and without apparent rational explanation. The individual facing the unknown. Inevitably the need arises to resolve the situation somehow, to reconcile what was and what is, yesterday with today, the past with the future, the here and there. How, then, to deal with this new reality and reconcile one's own identity? This resolution does not occur very quickly, nor can it occur at the speed with which the new reality is introduced; rather it must go through a process, often a long one. Within this process we can list the more general resolutions or alternatives, based on the use of language or linguistic expression as a measurement of the resolution or reconciliation of one's identity in the framework of the new situation and as opposed to the situation and identity left behind. This process leads to three possible resolutions: *Assimilation, Rejection,* or *Coexistence.*

Assimilation

Assimilation (also coined as the OTHER identity) is based on a complete metamorphosis in which the individual becomes part of the new world, system, culture and language. Chilean expatriate and writer Ariel Dorfman, born in Argentina and now a U.S. citizen and distinguished professor of literature at Duke University, describes this alternative:

> One strategy, of course, is assimilation: The migrant seeks to become an integral part of the new society, tries to forget or hide the mother tongue, wants to blur the accent, fantasizes that all bonds to the past can be cut, makes believe the dead are really, entirely dead. And if the originating migrant cannot always do this—because languages cannot be cast off like old socks—there is always the reverie that this full status in the new society will materialize with the children or, eventually, the grandchildren, conjecturing that some acquiescent offspring will overcome the curse of a bilingual, duplicated existence (Dorfman 2003, 31).

This assimilation strategy is one of the extremes in which people strive to achieve a unique identity (as opposed to a dual or bifurcated identity), a kind of clean slate, a starting over, a reinventing of oneself. This strategy requires a conscious, active, painful, and almost torturous practice that forces or demands that the individual undergo a process, the sole goal of which is full assimilation into the new culture and mastery of the language. This would be like cutting the tree at the trunk and grafting the shoots. In this endeavor, people actively or passively seek to merge with or blend into the new culture. This was the strategy assumed by large migratory waves that arrived in the United States at the beginning of the 20th century from countries such as Italy and Poland. It is worth noting that when a newcomer arrives with family members, they often prohibit speaking the mother tongue.

The idea is to cut all ties with the past, since the person convinces themself that they have come to stay, and in this way they undergo a painful process of learning, transformation, and denial: they transform into the OTHER identity, which is equivalent to undertaking a monolingual life. This strategy leads to name changes: the former Pedro becomes Peter, Juan becomes Johnny, María becomes Mary, Ramón becomes Raymond, and there will eventually be children named Washington or with the surname Smith or the like. However, this strategy has been in decline over the years as there is a greater acceptance and promotion of diverse ideas, which little by little is blurring the old Melting Pot doctrine by which everyone could morph, blend, and be part of the American casserole. This was the strategy used most often by families and individuals who came to the United States as part of the waves of migration spurred by World War I, the Great Depression, and World War II. Cases of migrants from the Spanish-speaking Caribbean island countries corresponding to those waves and causes have been poorly documented.

Rejection

Rejection (also referred to as the SINGULAR identity) is the other side of the assimilation coin and is the opposite extreme. Here the individual assumes a self-preservation strategy by refusing to accept the culture, system, and language of the new world. Ariel Dorfman explains this "rejection model" as follows:

The opposite of this solution [the assimilation strategy] is what could be called the rejectionist model: I have seen

Chilean compatriots of mine who, twenty-five years after they were first banished from their land, continue to stubbornly refuse to learn more than a few words of the host country's language, their faces and their hearts nostalgically fixed on their remote country, their tongues repeating colloquialisms that, in fact, have fallen out of use back home. It is not necessarily a tactic doomed to failure. They plan to return to Chile someday, to make the trip back, and indulge, therefore in that way, as do many Kurdish and Moroccan, Indonesian and Korean, Nigerian and Mexican emigrés in a similar situation, in a tactic of cultural survival that holds on to the native language as a pure and intact entity, a bridge, a down payment of that ticket home (Dorfman 2003, 31).

This Rejection Model strategy is perhaps the most fre-quent practice among Caribbean immigrants, and, whether practiced consciously or unconsciously, is seen mainly among adult emigrants who arrive and mostly settle in cities like Miami and New York (and in neighborhoods like Little Havana, El Barrio, and Washington Heights). This is, of course, survival by the path of least resistance. And here it is essential to note that this model is practiced regardless of the person's level of education, since these neighborhoods are overflowing with intellectuals whose English, after more than ten years in the United States, does not surpass the English of which Nicolás Guillén wrote in his poem "You don't know English": "Your English was from etrái guan / from etrái guan and guan tu tri." (Your English came from "strike one," strike one and one two three.)

In practice, in Dorfman's Rejection Model strategy, people do not assimilate the new culture or language because they refuse (either actively and consciously or passively and unconsciously) to learn, or learn only the minimum that is absolutely necessary to survive. They hope to one day return to their countries, thus clinging, almost irrationally, to a SINGU-LAR identity and a monolingual life. And although it seems like a choice (something the individual opts for), in reality and practice many times it is not. When adults must start over, the mechanical aspects of subsistence (working, eating, sleeping, etc.) are necessarily carried out by survival instinct. On the other hand, the intellectual aspects (learning another language, unpacking identity) are accomplished by the exercise of free will, by choice or conscious desire. And when necessity prevails over will, the outcome cannot be considered as the result of a choice or option.

By maintaining a single and monolingual identity, some intellectuals and writers will continue to have a certain validation in the country of origin but will always struggle to be included and considered. They cannot lower their guard for a moment or else they will be cast into oblivion: not published, not invited, not read, and not taken into account at all. Inevitably they will be considered, at best, under the label of "overseas" or "diaspora," and at worst as "outsiders" or even "traitors." And although it is much easier to stay current with the daily events of the country of origin than it was thirty years ago—since we can simply turn on our computers or look at our smart phones and have immediate access to all the newspapers and opinions about what is happening daily in our country of origin and submit Op-Eds or provide live commentary—this is achieved not without another sacrifice. That other sacrifice involves living blindly and ignoring the daily events of the immediate environment. It means not reading the *Wall Street Journal* or the *New York Times Magazine*. It means, in the worst case, not being able to give an intelligent opinion about what is happening around us in the local, state, or national contexts, whether about art, history, or politics. It means being absent within one's intellectual surroundings. It is, in the metaphorical sense, as if one had never left the homeland, as if one were living on an island, cut off from everything, but while on a continent.

The two strategies or alternatives outlined above—the Rejection Model and the Assimilation Strategy—represent the extremes and the monolingual identity of one side or the other: those who either adopt the OTHER identity and renounce their mother tongue, imposing on themselves and their children the monolingual identity of the host country; and those who, on the other hand, maintain a SINGULAR identity and exercise a monolingual life clinging to their mother tongue. Both options are monolingual: they contain the attraction of a complete, holistic, sole, undivided, immaculate identity, without bifurcations. They embody the attempt to avoid that kind of Janus existence that has plagued immigrants from all over and wherever they settle.

Dorfman notes that of the two options, the Assimilation strategy tends to be more frequent:

> Influential and effective institutions align themselves behind this monolingual alternative, first and foremost, the nation-state with all its history and resources brought to bear on creating and enforcing borders and boundaries, imposing them on geographies and bodies, on flags and hymns; as well as on syllables and relative clauses and interjections, identifying the nation with a language as a bulwark against foreign contamination, always alert to the need to control and homogenize its population in the name of security and internal order (Dorfman 2003, 32)[5].

Coexistence

The *Coexistence* of the two worlds is manifested in what I refer to from now on as the *Bilingual Alternative*. Although the *Assimilation* and *Rejection* alternatives represent the extremes of the *Other* and *Singular* identities, the *Bilingual Alternative* represents the center or middle ground of the migratory experience:

it is a third option—the bilingual and, by extension, bicultural alternative.

In the *Bilingual Alternative*, all the aforementioned factors are combined: the level of education of the newcomer; the individual's class or socio-economic position in their country of origin; the individual's age at the time of arrival; the reasons for leaving the origin country and venturing to (or being forced to) seek their fortune in another society, culture, and system; their attitudes toward the new host country (favorable, unfavorable, or even antagonistic); the occupation or job obtained upon arrival and whether or not they can practice in the same field in which they worked as part of the home country's national economy; the place (city or neighborhood) where they establish residence; plans for the future (immediate return or plans for a prolonged or indeterminate stay); and finally, how far away the home country is and what connections they have with that place (political, economic, social, and familial).

Within the *Bilingual Alternative* framework, the individual, either by choice or circumstances, begins what will eventually become a two-dimensional, bifurcated life; that is: a double existence of linguistic permeability in which the person can reach a state of not knowing for sure where is that place one calls "home" or "country" or "nation" or "homeland." This is the typical transtierro condition: those who live on that bridge that connects them with their multiple realities and identities, forced to declare allegiance to two countries, two languages, two cultures. It is living between and with the extremes of the OTHER and the SINGULAR identity.

The initial experience—both of extreme identities as a representation of the monolingual identity, and of the middle ground described in the *Bilingual Alternative*—represents surviving for some time (usually for the first few years of the immigrant experience within the new language and culture) with the daily need to live in two languages. Let's return to Ariel Dorfman, who expressed that daily necessity as follows:

They will not be able to avoid the need to live for many years in two languages, torn between the public dominant language, on the one hand, in which the police interrogate, the school principal complains about a child's conduct, bank accounts are opened and too often closed, groceries are bought, jobs are proffered, signs and advertisements are written, and on the other hand, the private and subjective set of words that keep the newcomers in touch with the old home and homeland and with the persons they once used to be, the persons they believe they still might once again become (Dorfman 2003, 30).

For those who had chosen, or those who had no choice but, to live under the *Bilingual Alternative,* to paraphrase Dorfman, life means "the need to live in two dimensions, pledge allegiance to two cultures, use one language to speak to the mail carrier and another to read the letters they bring from the homeland to your door." In other words, it means residing in a double existence; marrying two languages; being inhabited by two languages (that is, having them inside). Once the individual achieves "mastery" of the two languages and the "war in the throat" ceases, they can breathe a certain air of acceptance (not necessarily of trust, since the expression in both languages will always carry with it the doubt of acting, masking, and feeling like an impostor—without original agency,—the sense that they inhabit the bridge that connects the two realities and identities, but that they are not fully one thing nor the other, not on one side nor the other, neither here nor there). It is possible to find peace in the idea that, despite being a bifurcated person without a "homeland," there are obvious advantages to this hybridity and openness, since it is almost like carrying the victory medal of honor in the face of the long and devastating battle of emigration.

These days, and as the most powerful phenomenon in the history of humanity, both new immigrants and those who already inhabit the bridge of transtierro, have before them a new and powerful force, which can be both a tool and a trap: the Internet and the affordability of communication technologies.[6] This is something that immigrants from four or more decades ago did not have to deal with, but which today exerts a great influence making the *Bilingual Alternative* practically a necessity. Today's immigrants are in daily contact with the "old country" through email, newspapers, social media, etc. It is almost impossible not to maintain a "present" relationship with the "past." Situating this technological phenomenon among the influencing factors, we still cannot determine whether it would be beneficial or detrimental to the conditions that provide the need or development of the *Bilingual Alternative*. What we can say is that it is a very powerful tool to keep in continuous contact and that it lends itself as the means by which bilinguals and monolinguals coexist—in both languages and worlds simultaneously. The transterrado uses these means to communicate at the same time with the people who make up the circles of their double realities and their bifurcated identities, and thus we find the presence of bilingual messages, announcements, and communications. A quick glance at the *Facebook* profile of any transterrado will demonstrate the presence of both languages as a palpable sign of a two-dimensional existence, committed to two languages.

§§§

To summarize the three options discussed—the SINGULAR identity, the OTHER identity, and the *Bilingual Alternative*—I leave you with this poem by the "bilingual-American" and "Dominican-American" poet Rhina P. Espaillat:

Bilingual/Bilingüe

My father liked them separate, one there,
one here (allá y aquí), as if aware

that words might cut in two his daughter's heart
(el corazón) and lock the alien part

to what he was—his memory, his name
(su nombre)—with a key he could not claim.

"English outside this door, Spanish inside,"
he said, "y basta." But who can divide

the world, the word (mundo y palabra) from
any child? I knew how to be dumb

and stubborn (testaruda); late, in bed,
I hoarded secret syllables I read

until my tongue (mi lengua) learned to run
where his stumbled. And still the heart was one.

I like to think he knew that, even when,
proud (orgulloso) of his daughter's pen,

he stood outside mis versos, half in fear
of words he loved but wanted not to hear.

Bilingüe/Bilingual

A papá le gustaban separados, uno allá,
uno aquí (there and here), como si se diera cuenta

que las palabras podían cortar en dos el corazón de su hija
(the heart) y cerrarle el lado foráneo

a lo que él era —su memoria, su nombre
(his name)— con una llave que él no podría reclamar.

"Inglés de la puerta para afuera, español dentro",
dijo, "and that's it." ¿Pero quién puede dividirle

el mundo, la palabra (world and word)
a la infancia? Yo sabía hacerme la tonta

y testaruda (stubborn); tarde, en cama,
yo acumulaba sílabas secretas que había leído

hasta que mi lengua (my tongue) aprendió a correr
donde la suya tropezaba. Aun así el corazón era uno.

Quiero creer que él lo sabía, hasta cuando,
orgulloso (proud) de la pluma de su hija,

se quedó parado fuera de my verses, mitad temeroso
de palabras que amaba pero que no quería escuchar.

(poem translation into Spanish by Keiselim A. Montás)

CHAPTER 2

THE HISTORICAL FRAMEWORK of Spanish-speaking Caribbean Island Countries Emigration and Subsequent Linguistic Identities in Figures Who Represent Transtierro

THE SPANISH-SPEAKING CARIBBEAN ISLAND COUNTRIES AND THE UNITED STATES

Emigration from the Spanish-speaking Caribbean island countries to the United States dates back at least a century and a half. Throughout this history, countless groups of immigrants left their warm, tropical homelands to seek their fortune or save their lives in George Washington's homeland. There's a political nuance to the circumstances that led the first migratory groups to leave the Caribbean. With politics as the driving force, those first exoduses, so to speak, had the tenor of exile from the start and are worth contextualizing in a simplified relational framework. And while notable figures from Puerto Rico and Cuba emigrated or went into exile in the United States, this type of emigration from the Dominican Republic was toward Cuba and Puerto Rico or other Latin American countries, and not necessarily to the United States. In terms of mass migration, Dominicans emigrated to the United States much later than Cubans and Puerto Ricans—and for different reasons and under different circumstances.

Let's take a look at the framework of these three countries' relations with the United States. However cursory the analysis of emigration from the Spanish-speaking Caribbean island countries may be, the historical setting vis-à-vis the country of origin must always be considered in relation to the political context and the relationship of each country toward the United States as host country. By observing the interrelation of individual histories, political contexts, and the relationship between each nation and the host country we can delineate the migratory situations from Puerto Rico, Cuba, and the Dominican Republic. Hence, we can delineate guidelines to circumscribe the historical context as the thread connecting the current circumstances with their historical conjunctures.

During the 19th century, Caribbean emigration was mostly composed of political exiles from Cuba (José María Heredia, Cirilio Villaverde, José Martí, etc.) and from Puerto Rico (José Basora, Eugenio María de Hostos, Luis Muñoz Rivera, etc.). These individuals, opposed to Spanish colonialism in their countries, sought and found refuge in New York, where the freedom of the press in the United States allowed them to advance their anti-colonialist campaigns. From there, they continued to develop their political projects and advocate for the causes left behind. In these cases, life in New York became an obsessive struggle for the homeland from which they had been uprooted or forced to leave behind; their suitcases were never completely unpacked. On the other hand, emigration from the Dominican Republic to the United States during that century is almost non-existent. The Dominican political situation was completely different then: rather than a struggle against Spanish colonialism, it was an almost internal struggle to define an identity or nation. Juan Pablo Duarte studied English in New York, and there are traces of others who passed through the United States, such as Alejandro Angulo Guridi and Pedro Alejandro Pina, but there is no sojourn that could be described as transcendental, as would be the case of Juan Pablo Duarte when he was exiled in Venezuela, or of Alejandro Angulo Guridi in Cuba (Torres-Saillant, 2000).

The first half of the 20th century is marked by the North American occupation in these countries, which had a marked effect on the migratory context, colored by an inevitable connotation of cause and effect. This must also be viewed through the lens of each country's economic and political relationship with the United States. To that end, let's take a brief look at these individual relationships. First and foremost, Cuba and Puerto Rico's liberation from Spanish colonialism was part of the resolution of the wars for independence as stipulated in the 1898 Treaty of Paris, according to which Spain renounced all sovereignty and property rights over Cuba, and ceded the island of Puerto Rico to the United States, along with Guam and the Philippines.

§§§

Puerto Rico

We can begin by highlighting some key moments in the relationship between Puerto Rico and the United States: first, the occupation of Puerto Rico in 1898; second, the Jones Act of 1917, which declared the island as "territorial or American" and granted U.S. citizenship to Puerto Ricans; and third, the declaration of the island as a Commonwealth in 1952. These events gave Puerto Rico a drastically different status from Cuba and the Dominican Republic, and removed impediments to immigration procedures and legal issues, thus granting Puerto Ricans migratory freedom. Therefore, one can speak of "migratory waves" from Puerto Rico to the United States, which include the so-called *First and Second Migratory Waves* and *The Great Migration*.

The *First Migratory Wave* covers the years 1899 to 1901

and was characterized by the emigration of agricultural workers who sought better working conditions and who were promised a better quality of life; about six thousand went to work on the sugar cane plantations in Hawaii, which was already a U.S. territory. The *Second Migratory Wave* spans from 1917 to the late 1930s, and is characterized by the new citizenship status and the need for labor in the war-manufacturing industries, since the United States had entered World War I. Most of the emigrants from this second wave arrived in the 1920s and 1930s and settled in New York City. Finally, there is *The Great Migration*, which consists of the two decades between 1945 and 1965, and once again was a result of the need for labor after the end of World War II. According to data provided by the Puerto Rican Endowment for the Humanities[7],

> The State used various strategies to promote emigration. One was to increase air traffic between Puerto Rico and the United States and reduce ticket prices. Another was related to the diffusion of employment opportunities in the states of the Union, especially those in the northeast. Finally, it established standards of treatment that U.S. employers should offer Puerto Ricans who ventured to work there, especially seasonal workers. In addition, the government of Puerto Rico established offices under the Migration Division program in places like New York to offer information on jobs, housing and social services, and to attend to islanders' complaints on U.S. soil (Grupo Editorial EPRL, January 28, 2010).

However, freedom of migration, incentives, and legal status—serving as a kind of migratory facilitator—are not nec-essarily a magic bullet for an islander to feel equally at home in Reading, Pennsylvania, as in Mayagüez, Puerto Rico. Despite being U.S. passport holders, Puerto Rican immigrants have suffered as much as any other immigrants. The condition of separation and uprooting has been experienced in the same way, in terms of the aforementioned adaptation processes, as emigration from Cuba and the Dominican Republic or any other nation in a similar context.

§ § §

Cuba

The relationship between Cuba and the United States has been influenced by the U.S. occupation in Cuba when it was a so-called protectorate from 1898 to 1902, following Cuba's independence from Spain and during the establishment of the first Cuban government. The second occupation took place in 1906, then in 1917, and again in 1922. These occupations were followed by dictatorships and corrupt governments that would lead to the Cuban Revolution in 1959 and Fidel Castro's rise to power. During the 1930s and under the dictatorship of Gerardo Machado y Morales, Alejo Carpentier left for Paris and Lino Novás Calvo went to Madrid. During the dictatorship of Fulgencio Batista there were also many exiles among writers and intellectuals, several of whom returned after the start of the Cuban Revolution. But the Cuban Revolution itself has produced the largest number of exiles from the island. According to a PBS article on Fidel Castro, titled "Cuban Exiles in America" in the historical series *The American Experience*, there were four waves of emigration after the revolution:

> Since the triumph of Fidel Castro's revolution in 1959, there has been a steady influx of Cubans into the United States, punctuated by four significant waves: 1959–1962; 1965–1974; 1980; and 1993–5. Each wave has reached deeper into the layers of Cuban society, from the wealthy

in the 1960s to the dwellers of Havana's squalid inner-city neighborhoods in the 1990s.[8]

The first "wave" primarily comprised the first Cubans opposed to the Revolution; among them were writers such as Hilda Perera and Carlos Alberto Montaner, and Carlos Montenegro. The second wave stemmed from President Lyndon B. Johnson's "Freedom Flights" that "welcomed" a quarter-million Cubans to the United States by 1974, including Guillermo Cabrera Infante and Matías Montes Huidobro. The third wave was the famous exodus of the "marielitos," from April to September 1980, when some 125,000 Cubans were brought by boat from the port of Mariel to Florida; José Triana and Reinaldo Arenas were among them. After the collapse of the Soviet Union, the Cuban economy shrank by approximately 40%, leading to great scarcity in an era deemed the Special Period. The fourth wave corresponds to the so-called *balseros* (rafters); during those years, desperate people took to the seas on anything that floated.

§§§

Dominican Republic

There were numerous U.S. military interventions in the Dominican Republic as well, beginning with the 1903 intervention, then in 1914, also the remarkable occupation from 1916 to 1924, and finally, from 1965 to 1966. In 1918, during the 1916–1924 occupation, Rafael Leónidas Trujillo enlisted in the National Army and was trained by the U.S. Marines. Trujillo went on to rule the nation by force and intimidation with a dictatorship that extended from 1930 until his assassination in 1961. In 1966, after the invasion that occurred as a result of the April 1965

Revolution, the U.S. installed the administration of Joaquín Balaguer who had been a puppet president under Trujillo and the greatest apologist of the dictatorship. These interventions also left a trail of corruption and dictatorships in the Dominican Republic.

Emigration from the Dominican Republic has been sporadic and is in no way comparable to the mass departures from Puerto Rico in the first half of the 20th century, or from Cuba in the decades after the Revolution. Pedro and Max Henríquez Ureña were among the first Dominican emigrants; after finishing their secondary schooling in Santo Domingo, the brothers were sent by their father to study at Columbia University in New York City. Their sister, Salomé Camila Henríquez Ureña, joined the faculty at Vassar College, in New York's Hudson Valley. The lesser-known Virginia de Peña de Bordas also studied in the U.S. in the 1920s. The migratory explosion from the Dominican Republic to the U.S. began to pick up in the last quarter of the 20th century, peaking in the 1980s, when the number of Dominicans legally entering the United States from 1981 to 1990 surpassed all sending countries in the Western Hemisphere, with the exception of México (Rumbaut 1992, 288). This makes Dominican emigration to the U.S. the most recent among the Spanish-speaking countries of the Caribbean.

As we have seen, the first three decades of the 20th century produced many emigrants from Puerto Rico to the United States, as well as countless political exiles from Cuba and some from the Dominican Republic. The emigration from the Dominican Republic and Cuba at the beginning of the century was led by the wealthy and/or intellectual classes; the Puerto Rican emigrants were primarily agricultural workers leaving en masse. Some left the Dominican Republic as exiles, while others were sent by their parents to study abroad (generally to the U.S., Cuba, and European countries). This practice was understood as a way to save children from compulsory exile, political persecution, or death.

During the important decade from 1952 to 1962, in the Spanish-speaking Caribbean island countries, a series of events opened doors and gave way, on the one hand, to "transtierro emigration" driven by economics or as a desired or actively sought condition as opposed to exile, which is purely political or ideological as previously articulated. And on the other hand, a new phenomenon of mass political exile began, which, over time and due to its ongoing nature, became a form of trans-tierro. In 1952, Puerto Rico became a Commonwealth; in 1959, the Cuban Revolution triumphed; and in 1961, in the Dominican Republic, the dictatorship ended with the assassination of Rafael Leónidas Trujillo.

§§§

LANGUAGE IN THE LITERARY PRODUCTION OF THE CARIBBEAN TRANSTIERRO

Given all these waves of emigration—some haphazard, some scattered, others massive—today the imprint of the Spanish-speaking Caribbean island countries is well-represented and continues to grow in North American life and society. In this imprint or testimony, the conditions of exile and transtierro have been conjugated, and sometimes fused and confused. Those first exiles who arrived in the United States decades ago and have stayed for so long, even as the political circumstances that caused their exile begin to dissipate, are evidence that they exist as transterrados rather than as exiles.

This has resulted in the formation of a myriad of linguistic identities, depending on the country of origin and its historical circumstances (as a stand-in for the reasons and duration of their presence in the host country). These linguistic identities can be analyzed through their respective written manifestations if we consider the literary production of representative figures from these diasporas (a term which I will address in the next chapter). Therein we can point out, with a certain level of precision, the instances where identity options manifest, using language as a touchstone. This is evidenced in the literary production and creative work of these representative figures and their corresponding linguistic identities as monolingual (in English or in Spanish) or bilingual. These writers, each at their own time, defined (and continue to define) their creative identity by choosing to write in one language or the other. Or perhaps they are only able to write in one or the other, or some are able to write in both, or they opt for the hybrid bifurcation of bilingualism and translation.

Thousands of people with citizenship status have left Puerto Rico to work in the United States. As I have pointed out, the 1950s through 1965 made up what is known as *The Great Migration*. By then, people commonly traveled by plane, which bears the mark of a short trip (not an arduous crossing), and consciously or unconsciously leaves alight the flame of an almost instantaneous return. This migratory wave spawned the great Nuyorican movement, which is recognized and accepted as the first true literary movement of the Puerto Rican diaspora. A key representative is the late Tato Laviera (1950–2013), whose poetic oeuvre fluctuated between English, Spanish, and Spanglish, as a living example of that duality of inhabiting two languages. There are other figures who developed outside of established literary trends or movements, such as Lourdes Vázquez, who chose to write in Spanish and be translated, despite having developed a full command of English through her education and professional life.

Following the Cuban Revolution, there were two migratory streams from Cuba to the United States: those who left shortly after the Revolution in a political exile or escape (namely the wealthy; and if not "wealthy," those with the financial means to leave); and later the masses, who left during

the "Freedom Flights." Among those exiles, or their future generations of transterrados, is the poet José Kozer, recipient of the
2013 Pablo Neruda Ibero-American Poetry Prize, who left Cuba
at age twenty and underwent a very interesting process, at the
end of which he decided to write exclusively in Spanish, and to
translate from English into Spanish. Kozer is perhaps one of
most vocal writers about the transition from his native country
to the United States, linguistically speaking. In a 2007 interview
published in *Jacket Magazine*, Kozer recounted:

> ...at age twenty I moved from Cuba, not to Miami where
> I would have ended up in a ghetto speaking in Spanish,
> but to New York during a time, the 1960s, when there
> weren't a lot of Latinos in New York ... I began to lose my
> Spanish, and I wanted to write, and suddenly three or
> four years after, I'm only speaking English, no Spanish,
> and when I tried to write... I could not write because I
> didn't have the language anymore; the instrument was
> gone...
> English is not my language; it's not my native language;
> Spanish, which is my native language, I'm losing — what
> do I do?
> It became like a nightmare, a nightmare where you have
> to add other factors; for instance, I started drinking a lot,
> became somewhat of an alcoholic; I had a lousy mar-
> riage; it was a disastrous marriage; I was very poor, no
> money — complex story, you know the story of an
> immigrant who's also Bohemian, who was also trying to
> earn a living, to adjust to a new society, a changing life,
> and I was also having a lot of fun — and in that situation,
> at one point, I realized that I was moving into a no-man's
> land where I would have no language whatsoever. And
> if I'm a poet, what's going to happen?
> So at that point, something happened within me — I
> think the Spanish language was stuck in my stomach,

and through alcohol, it became released; it came out; it came out and I started writing again in Spanish, poems and poems and poems and poems, and I got into my profession teaching Spanish and Spanish literature…[9]

Achy Obejas arrived from Cuba at age six and was educated in English, and tacitly maintains her linguistic roots. She became a journalist and writes creatively in English, and today she also translates writers such as Junot Díaz and Wendy Guerra.

With Trujillo's fall in 1961, people in the Dominican Republic went from fleeing the tyrant to fleeing his avengers and, later, the political and economic repression of the Balaguer regime. The mass exodus of Dominicans began in the 1970s; they travelled to Venezuela and the Lesser Antilles in search of fortune and economic betterment. By the end of the 1970s, the United States became the new destination and Dominicans left en masse, either legally or on makeshift boats, peaking in the 1980s. This quasi-desired exodus (since traveling abroad became fashionable), makes the Dominican community the "youngest" presence in the United States; nonetheless, we do have some literary representatives.

Rhina Espaillat arrived in the U.S. at age seven in 1939, when her family fled the Trujillo dictatorship. From a very early age, she was an excellent poet in English. After several decades dedicated to her family and her profession as an educator, she reappeared on the American literary scene as part of the Formalist movement in the early 1990s. Since then, she has not stopped writing and publishing in English and Spanish, and she is considered the most prominent Spanish translator of Robert Frost's poetry. We also have the aforementioned cases of Julia Álvarez, whose family fled the Trujillo dictatorship and settled in the U.S. in 1960, when she was ten; and Junot Díaz, who arrived at age six in 1974. Both were educated in English, and therefore they write in English, but their works are indisputably

Dominican. There are also more recently arrived writers, among them: Viriato Sención (1941–2012), the award-winning José Acosta, Marianela Medrano, and Josefina Báez, among many others. We also have those born in the U.S. such as Angie Cruz, a rising star born in New York City, who writes in English, but is oh-so-*dominicana*.

Given its incipient production and other persistent circumstances, the literature produced by Dominicans in the United States is little-known and the options for promotion and publishing have been limited. The success of authors such as Junot Díaz and Julia Álvarez has shone a spotlight on Dominican literature. Thanks to several anthologies published by Franklin Gutiérrez and Daisy Cocco de Filippis, Dominican literature has become more visible and accessible to readers and academic centers in the United States. Among these anthologies: *Diccionario de la literatura dominicana* (2004 and 2010); *Antología histórica de la poesía dominicana del siglo XX* (1995); *Niveles del imán* (anthology of Dominican poets in New York, 1983); *Historias de Washington Heights y otros rincones del mundo* (anthology of short stories, 1994); and *Poems of Exile and Other Concerns: A Bilingual Selection of Poems Written by Dominicans in the United States* (1988).

The cited examples, together with the brief political-migratory history, lead us to the present human condition that I have defined as transtierro. The daily lives of a Dominican bodega owner in the South Bronx, a Cuban merchant in Union City, or a Puerto Rican taxi driver in Chicago have commonalities and reveal the same linguistic identities represented in the literary production of the intellectuals and writers of the Caribbean transtierro. Despite divergent situations, eras, and motives for emigration, they inevitably share a common cultural and linguistic heritage, which is unleashed in a literary production that is faithful to the different political and economic realities that make up the respective circumstances that converted the emigrant to a transterrado.

How would today's transterrado define their condition as an inhabitant of that bridge connecting multiple realities and identities? We have said enough about the theorization of this condition. Here is one answer to that question, from one transterrada (Lourdes Vázquez) to another (Madeline Millán[10]) as recounted in a 2013 post on Vázquez's blog, *lookingazul*:

—Lourdes Vázquez: Two countries, one memory. How do you manage it?

—Madeline Millán: Today, it's snowing in Manhattan and I've got "the blues." Two countries and one memory. I once had a memory of the past. I kept memories of my ancestors, of a recent past. But I only have my father's surname, one grandmother, and a bicycle. Everything else is fragile, fading like a candle in the wind.

What is a country if I associate it with the family that I lost?

Our colonial state is painful to me; our language is invaded by the otherness of English. I think of Hostos' remains that may never return to his homeland because he conditioned it upon a free country. The island has been and will always be a country of sun and wonder. Once, in an interview for *El Nuevo Día*, they asked me if I would consider going back. I don't want to return nor stay anywhere. In Lisbon I discovered, by reading a poem by Sophia de Mello Breyner with the line "my land is the sea," that, yes, perhaps the sea is my country. It's not two countries and one memory. I'm no longer from a country and the memory of the things to come matters more to me than the memory of the things I don't want to remember. If you like, I'm from the Caribbean, or from Valparaíso, Paris, México, Lisbon, Andalusia, Alphabet City, from anywhere that I've been happy.[11]

CHAPTER 3

DIASPORA: What Separates Us? What Brings Us Together?

Here I would like to pause and touch on the concept of "diaspora" in terms of its applicability to immigrant groups from the Spanish-speaking Caribbean island countries. Many people, particularly among the Dominican intelligentsia, dis-agree that the term applies to us, that we are not or do not comprise any diaspora. Let's start by doing away with the idea that "diaspora" is a physical place (such as Little Havana, El Barrio, or Washington Heights). Rather, it is any group of people wherever they may be—whether they were the first family to migrate, or a single individual—who have left behind their place of origin and settled in another place while maintaining their identity and connection with that original place. We need only to verify the meaning of the word in any dictionary. According to English language *Merriam-Webster* dictionary, "diaspora" has two basic definitions: 1. the Jews living outside Palestine or modern Israel; 2. the movement, migration, or scattering of a people away from an established or ancestral homeland.

The *Dictionary of the Royal Academy of the Spanish Language* (*Diccionario de la lengua española, Real Academia Española* [*RAE*]) (*Twenty-Second Edition*) offers similar definitions. The argument is simple: we *are* diaspora, since we are part of the dispersion of a human group that has abandoned its place of origin and maintains a real or imaginary connection with that left-behind place. If the term-deniers' argument is based solely on the first definition, it is obvious that it is not fully applicable to our case; but relying on only one of the two definitions of the term is faulty logic for it is equally applicable to both definitions, and the second definition completely encompasses us as the dispersion of a human group that has abandoned its place of origin or homeland and that maintains, as we transterrados do, a living, fluid, strong—and sometimes growing—connection with that land.

I propose that the term is applicable to situations concerning even a single individual. I justify this argument in the free interpretation of the expression "dispersion of human groups": from "dispersion" we extract "disperse" which is "to separate and disseminate what was or used to be gathered." It seems pertinent to clarify that this argument of including a single person in this definition began as an answer to the question that I and many migrants have asked ourselves, having experienced a similar situation: When we believe or know ourselves to be the only person (not a group, but an individual) in a place far from our origins, do we constitute a diaspora? In these circumstances, anecdotal evidence seems to indicate that the individual comes to feel more connected to that original place than ever. Some people admit to drawing a little flag on the calendar on national holidays or listening to their home country's national anthem on Independence Day, or to having been overcome by melancholy and burst into tears in front of strangers when something has touched a heartstring of the national instrument that they carry within.

Scattered around the world, alone or in groups, do we stop being from where we are from to be only the separation from what we *were*? We must ask ourselves: And what about what we were? Was that not enough to continue being part of that which today is dispersed and making a life elsewhere? These questions do not propose or seek answers, they simply pose the question in the context of what constitutes a diaspora, rhetorically, because within the condition of transtierro, distance and separation do not obviate our identity.

From that homeland we venture out: divided efforts, partaking in activities that refract our attention like colors spun off haphazardly in multiple directions, far away, exiled, transterrado, diasporated, somehow we remain connected. We are still close, either because of that continued connection with our homeland through memory, experience, skin color, hair, and accent in the new language, or in maintaining our native language as if it were our homeland, our birthplace. And what is "homeland" (*patria*)? Let's return to affinity, to language, to the dictionary:

—*Patria*: f. Native or adopted land ordered as a nation, to which the human being feels bound by legal, historical and emotional ties (*RAE*)

—*homeland*: 1. native land: Fatherland; 2. a state or area set aside to be a state for a people of a particular national, cultural, or racial origin (*Merriam-Webster*)

And now we return to a duality: on the one hand being separated from the place of origin, juxtaposed with the adopted place. On the other, feeling linked by legal, historical, and emotional ties to two nations. And in the practical and the day-to-day: we commit to living in two cultural and linguistic spaces —"water from two rivers," after the title of a book by Rhina Espaillat. Separation is impossible for us, and our duality influences our creative practice, the language we speak, the way we communicate with people we love, our profession or education, identity, memory, real or imaginary distance, our longing to return, etc. Yet, the privilege of being part of the diaspora or the transtierro cannot be granted to those who cut themselves off from the past, change their names, bury their language, their culture and their customs, deny their roots, and forfeit their identity.

CHAPTER 4

PERSONAL MANIFESTATIONS of the Bilingual/Bicultural Alternative vis-à-vis Identity and Creativity

I want to move on to my personal account of how the bicultural and *Bilingual Alternative* has manifested in me, from my perspective and life experience, and how it has influenced my identity and my creative work as a transterrado.

INTRODUCTION TO ENGLISH

I was sixteen when I arrived in New York City with no real notion of English. I had taken English classes in the Dominican Republic, where English was taught just as Spanish, French, and other "foreign" languages are taught in schools in the United States, but with one small and significant difference: my teachers in the Dominican Republic did not speak English. This is not the case in the United States, where language teachers are often native speakers of the languages they teach. When I enrolled in high school, the academic counselor gave me a test to see what level of English as a Second Language (ESL) I would enroll in. He asked me: "Where were you born?" And I looked at him with such a bewildered expression on my face that he said, nodding: "Level 1."

I was enrolled in the second year of high school (the 10th grade) in the bilingual high school program at John Bowne

High School in Flushing, NY, a school that, at that time, had a diverse student body representing 52 countries. Reflecting on this experience, I applaud the existence of that bilingual program, which allowed me to continue my education in Spanish at an appropriate level for my intellect while acquiring the level of literacy and acculturation I needed in English. Since then, I have been an advocate for bilingual education, offering my personal experience relative to my cousins', who emigrated a decade before me when there were no bilingual education programs in their public schools. They were put into "Special Education" classes and labeled as mentally disabled simply because they did not speak English.

From ESL Level 1, I progressed to Level 3, and two years later, the first term of my senior year, I was already in a mainstream literature class. As I progressed in my language acquisition, I had my first regular class in English: Chemistry (of all subjects, Chemistry!). Everyone mocked my pronunciation of "ke-mis-tri." Even so, I kept raising my hand in class, and Mr. Chasnoff (to whom I am grateful), with singular patience kept giving me the opportunity to participate. One classmate (Alex) bullied me the entire semester for participating in class, and, above all, for speaking with a strange accent, and I think also for giving the correct answer most of the time. Around that time, I also had to take choir class and another classmate (Roberto) tormented me every day, constantly making fun of my accent and yelling at me to speak English.

Not only was I a "know-it-all," but I also had a strong accent (and I still do, which I always forget) and my circle of friends was limited to two groups: 1) those who, like me, were also sailing in the turbulent seas of the new language and culture; and 2) the "Americans" I had befriended in the Student Union. This marked the beginning of my linguistic and cultural dichotomy, and of the subsequent hybridity of the transition. I had two sets of monolingual friends—those who only spoke Spanish and, like me, were navigating in the open seas of the new culture; and my "American friends" who only spoke English. I also had other friends with whom I had to communicate in "broken English" because they did not come from Spanish-speaking countries but they were finding their own footing in the new culture and language. It was evident that for immigrant students who already spoke English well (Alex was Russian; Roberto was Ecuadorian; Mabel was Honduran) it was not popular to hang out with students like me.

Even my neighbors from across the street who had never even acknowledged my existence—the Castillo siblings from Colombia, who rode the school bus with me every day—only ever spoke to me after the graduation ceremony in which I, as salutatorian, had given the welcome speech to our class of 658 graduates. The sister (Claudia) approached me and said: "I didn't know you were so smart!" And from then on the brother (William) always greeted me when he saw me on the street.
About ten years later, I ran into Mabel (RIP), with whom I had been madly in love—or as they say in good Dominican: "aficia'o"—on Broadway in Lower Manhattan. An electric shock ran down my spine when I saw her, and without hesitation I said, "Hi Mabel, remember me?" And she replied, astonished: "Oh my God, you speak English now!"

And this was my introduction to English.

§ § §

RELATIONSHIP WITH LANGUAGE AND WRITING

Acquiring English brought a new perspective to my relationship with language and writing. I have had a special fascination with words since childhood, and I have known ever since that language was perhaps the most powerful of human abilities. I suppose that's where my penchant for writing as a means of creative expression comes from. Words such as 'permeable,' 'commitment,' 'reiterate,' 'parallel,' 'reason,' fascinated me since I was little. I wrote my first verses (at least the ones I still have) when I was eight or nine years old. I also attempted to cofound a newspaper called *El Crítico*—a friend would do the illustrations, and I would write the articles. We did a piece entitled "El apagón" (The Blackout) that criticized the national newspapers for predicting a general blackout, which didn't happen, during the vote count for a presidential election.

It was with this same fascination with words that I began to learn this new language, and with equal curiosity I began to discover words in English. The word 'surface,' which I used in an essay on public transportation in New York City, helped get me selected for an interview for a scholarship to an English immersion program. In the essay I used that word to indicate my preference for buses, or surface transportation, as opposed to the subway, since you can see the city through the large bus windows as if you were watching a movie screen. As part of that entrance process, I was asked to write another free-topic essay, and I wrote about what it had meant to me to leave my town, school, and friends to live a new life in the United States. I used the word "contrast" to bridge the life I had left behind and my new life. It seems they were quite impressed with the use of that particular word; I got the scholarship and spent that summer, while still in high school, in the American Language Program at Columbia University, learning English along with the then Vice-Consul of Japan.

Throughout high school, I continued to write poems in Spanish and to play with my newly discovered language skills. For the first time, I tried to keep a diary (in Spanish). Curiously, during one of my father's brief attempts to live in the United States, I wrote my journal entries in English (so that he could not read them). My father ultimately returned to live in our warm Dominican homeland—there he remained a complete person and not simply an almost invisible being with no voice or vote, or another mute immigrant whom no one knew, and whose opinion didn't matter to anyone in the United States.

§§§

THE *BILINGUAL ALTERNATIVE*

Unlike my father, I stayed. Given the circumstances of my arrival, amongst the options facing newcomers I discussed in Chapter 1, the *Bilingual Alternative* approach was most fitting to me. This manifests itself in practical areas of daily living that happen in both English and Spanish (working, shopping, talking with my family, sharing with friends, etc.), in the realm of creative expression (which I practice almost exclusively in Spanish), and in the duality of being a guest in two languages.

In a practical sense, I have an obligation to communicate in both languages: my father, my sister and her family live in the Dominican Republic and are monolingual. My mother is in New York City, and only speaks Spanish even after more than thirty-five years there; she is the living example of the Rejection Alternative: she has only learned what is absolutely necessary to survive here and holds onto hope of retiring in her native land. My two brothers in New York are bilingual and we communicate in English: one, who also arrived young and finished his education in New York, and went on to be a professor in the English Department at Columbia University; and the other was born in the U.S. and speaks, but cannot read or write, Spanish. I also have a large extended family and circle of friends, some bilingual, others monolingual—all over the linguistic, geographic, and cultural spectrum. For example, when I moved from New York to another city, of course I wanted my family and friends to have my new address. But would I send two emails (one in English and one in Spanish) or just one that was bilingual? Could I send a single monolingual e-mail? No, I could not, because I have a living relationship with both worlds, culturally and linguistically speaking. And, yes, I could well send two messages (one in English and one in Spanish), but would it be practical? No, and it would also be like dividing my loved ones, and, to paraphrase Rhina Espaillat: the heart cannot be divided.

§§§

CREATIVITY

The need to communicate in both languages also applies to the creative realm, which has its own bifurcation: I communicate in one language, English, to earn a living; and I communicate in another, Spanish, to live. Let me explain: Since high school, and in order to earn a living, I have worked in the Public Safety (private security and law enforcement) field, which demands an excessive amount of writing. Although it can be considered "professional/business writing," it still demands discipline and creativity. a lot of telling and recounting of events, writing of directives, rules and regulations, and detailed standard operating procedures and manuals. In this area I have had to confront the fact that I speak with an accent; therefore I have had to be very conscious in my writing, as if in it I was trying to compensate for any linguistic or communicative imbalance. I have done this knowingly, because my 'recipients,' easily driven by irrational prejudice against anything foreign, could call into question my intellectual abilities based on my spoken accent. And I have put this to the test: I once served in a position where I reported to the Director of Administration, who had to approve all communications from the department and who, in turn, reported to the vice president (who was a terrible writer). At first, the Director would carefully scrutinize any memorandum I wrote, and flag the most insignificant trifles, while the vice president wrote atrocities. One day when two communiqués came out (one from me and the other from the vice president), mine was approved after he asked me to change a word and a punctuation mark. I took my directive and the vice president's, with the twenty-seven errors that I had found and marked in red ink and presented myself in the director's office. After that, the director would not let anything written by anyone (especially the vice president) go out without first having me check it.

I mention this episode to point out that I have had to demonstrate on paper that even though I *speak* with an accent —which in many cases like mine makes us permanent foreigners in the new country—I do not *think* with an accent. That perception is an affliction of those who judge the ability and intelligence of others based solely on something as superficial as an accent. When that happens, they are the ones who think with the clumsiness of an accent. This is one of the greatest sources of discrimination that immigrants face. And of course, my awareness of this phenomenon also exerts its influence on my oral ability: when I have to speak in public, which happens frequently, the more aware I am of the process, the more subject I am to twisting my tongue and RRROOOLLLing my r's and butchering my words. After all, I am also human, and one of our self-defense mechanisms is to turn inwards—to ourselves, to our loved ones, to what we know and where we feel safe. It is like returning to the linguistic homeland. I also tend to compensate by using analogies and synonyms: I have also developed a keen sense of words and their connections to each other. In writing, as opposed to speaking, I have much more control over correcting mistakes and more opportunity for autocorrection. Written expression allows for editing, changing words, and removing and adding sentences, unlike spontaneous oral expression where the fear of error and the impulse for autocorrection compete, simultaneously, with utterances.

Moving on from the use of language as a practical tool to earn a living, I turn to that other exercise, creativity, which is this fundamental need to communicate, create, write, live. And that is where creative expression comes in, and in my case, it happens almost exclusively in Spanish. In that expression, out of necessity, I express my life as I live it: as a person who incarnates the *Bilingual Alternative*. To satisfy that need, I made a conscious decision to maintain a connection with the culture and language I grew up in. I needed to earn a living in English, so rather than abandon my other language I opted to use it for actual living: I write in Spanish, and I write every day. That completes me as a whole person, and defines me. My creative desire is that internal force that pushes me to mold words to try to tell a story with precision, to evoke a specific sensation or reaction whether in prose or verse, in regulations or processes. Satisfying this creative need through the practice of writing is what forms, creates, or makes the writer. If I had not made that decision to cultivate creative writing in Spanish, I think I would still be a writer today, but not a bilingual writer. I think I can say that I do "creative writing" in Spanish; although, as I said, I also write creatively in English, albeit much less frequently.

§§§

TRANSLATION

Living this transtierro condition and using words and languages as tools for creative expression also implies the constant need for translation—to be read and understood in both languages. Within this need to communicate either through "professional" or "creative" writing, translation is the daily bridge to be crossed toward that vital viability of those of us who embody the *Bilingual Alternative*. Given my fascination with words and language, translation, while undoubtedly a challenge, is an almost pleasant and enjoyable practice for me. Translation work has a palpable flavor that can almost be savored on the palate, in the ears, and in the brain. Translation is the attempt to transfer a thought from one cultural and linguistic register to another in such a way that the result does not betray the original, while at the same time evoking a similar register in its translated form that can be read, accepted, and perceived as original.

Using the term coined by the Cuban sociologist Rubén Rumbaut, "Generation 1.5"[12], to refer to something similar to what I define here as the *Bilingual Alternative*, but in the strict context of exile, Gustavo Pérez Firmat, also Cuban, writes: "People in Generation 1.5 are translation artists" (Pérez Firmat, 5), in the sense that they have the advantage of coming and going, moving from one culture to another and from one linguistic register to another. Pérez Firmat sees this as an advantage that the 1.5-ers have, in contrast to their first-generation parents or second-generation children born here, since both of the latter have cultural and linguistic access to a single world (the parents to the "old" and the children to the "new"). Rumbaut does not see this as entirely positive, since he affirms that the 1.5-ers in many ways end up being marginalized in both the old and new worlds, not belonging completely to one or the other (Rumbaut, 61). Although they clearly differ in this regard, I have to agree with both: with Rumbaut, since one can indeed become an outsider in both places, and with Pérez Firmat, regarding the advantage of linguistic and cultural permeability that can make us successful in both cultures.

However, I do disagree with Rumbaut and Pérez Firmat in that both advocate implicitly for an identity without bifurcations, personified either in the first generation as members of the "old" world, or the second generation as members of the "new" world. In this sense, the categorization of immigrants into generations 1, 1.5, and 2 oversimplifies the phenomenon of immigration, and excludes the process of acculturation and the condition of existing between both cultures and two lands that any newcomer inevitably experiences for some time. It also assumes that those born here have an almost complete break with the past. Pérez Firmat wrote:

> My parents, already in their seventies, have no other option than to be Cuban. No matter how many years they have lived off the island—and if they live long enough, the time will soon come when they will have lived longer in Miami than in Havana—they are as Cuban today as they were when they got off the ferry in 1960. My children, who were born in this country to Cuban parents, and in whom I have tried to instill some kind of Cubanness, are Americans from head to toe. They may not be "saved" from their Americanness any more or less than my parents can "save" themselves from their Cubanness … Like other second-generation immigrants, they [my children born in this country] maintain a connection with their parents' homeland, but it is a bond forged from my experiences and not theirs. For my children, Cuba is an enduring, perhaps charming, fable. Cuba is for them as ethereal as smoke, and as persistent as the smell of their grandfather's cigars (which are not even Cuban, but Dominican)" (Pérez Firmat, 5).

Well, although at the time that was the pattern of Cuban immigrants, due to their situation of exile, that has not been the constant with Dominicans or Puerto Ricans or any other group of immigrants in the last thirty years who have not had to carry the weight of political exile. My own daughter who by the time she was three years old had already traveled to the Dominican Republic three times, when asked where her grandfather lived, would answer "En Cambita Garbito." Once again I turn my gaze to the near future, and I speculate that with the changes in the relations between Cuba and the United States, parents (from Generations 1 and 1.5) will be able to return to Cuba, and come and go freely, reinforcing this lifestyle between lands, countries, homelands, homes, etc. without being entirely on one side or the other. And that will change the panorama of some second-generation Cubans and, without a doubt, of Cubans who arrived in the last two or three decades and their descendants (even if they were born in this country).

Back to translation, I would like to reflect briefly on the question of whether I translate myself. Many people, particularly monolinguals, associate self-translation with trivialities that are revealed in their questions, such as: "Do you first think about what you are going to say in Spanish and then translate it into English?" Or the proverbial question: "Do you think in English or in Spanish?" These are questions that, without meaning to offend, seem childish and silly to me. We think in order to learn something, and once it has been learned, it comes automatically, like driving a car or tying shoelaces.

Language is not thought *a priori*, but the other way around: language is used to explain thought. Without the need for explanations or communication, language (which is a tool) would not exist. And going back to translation and the need to be understood (or explained) in two languages, when I reflect, I ask myself: Do I self-translate? And the most honest answer I can offer in this regard is that I don't, or sometimes I do, or I don't know... I have done impromptu translations of my literary work for friends, but I honestly believe that I should never put my name next to a piece of my published work that says "translated by the author" (although I would gladly appear as a collaborator). I believe this ambivalence is rooted in my vision of translation as a creative activity, as an activity of authorship—translation is a craft. I claim the creative position of authorship regarding my creative work and I firmly believe that the creative impulse manifests itself in its likeness and according to the medium available. In other words, a painting is not a photograph or a statue; paintings are created with paint, photography with a camera, and sculpture with various materials and tools. Similarly, writing is done according to the available tool for its effective materialization. For me, this can be in English or in Spanish, but I cultivate Spanish more as a creative tool. When claiming my role as author and presenting my written work, if I do it in both languages I will not name one as a translation of the other, rather both are products of my creative work. I can change the creative focus and target one audience or another, or present it as one or another creative manifestation of the same subject. I have collaborated on the translation of my work, and I will continue to do so, just as I have collaborated on the translation of other authors' work. Translation as a creative practice is fascinating to me, but I don't think I could credit myself as the translator of my own work, but as the author of another version of it.

Moving away from the field of creativity, I also want to address the notion or concept of identity in terms of the condition of hosting two languages. It is in this aspect of the *Bilingual Alternative* where the individual's dichotomy, duality, permeability, hybridity and bifurcation are most pronounced. Usually, one goes about their daily life without stopping to think about this duality unless it comes up in conversation, or when an opportunity for contrast illuminates this dichotomy. I can say that I lead a public life in English (the one that consumes most of my time), and that in order to maintain a connection with that other language, Spanish, I lead an inner, daily life in Spanish: I read in Spanish, I keep a journal in Spanish, I read both the *New York Times* and the *Listín Diario*. My diary is monolingual and when I am forced to write something in English, it appears in quotation marks as if they were not my words but someone else's, as if they were actually foreign; for example, I would write: "brunch," "laptop," "PC" —

words that do not have an immediate equivalent, and are part of the vocabulary acquired in the new language and culture, in quotes. I do this in my journal perhaps as an illusory way to somehow hold onto my primary unique identity; however, I know that they are but vestiges of that old identity since I am aware that time goes on.

Now, how does this dichotomy of living between two languages manifest? It does so in my relationships with the world and in the world's relationships with me. In relating to the world, as the host of two languages, Spanish is the language for my private life; my language of memory; the language that touches my heartstrings (I can easily be moved to tears by a song or a poem). It is my language for poetry and games of ambiguity, for passive resistance and silence, for whispers and murmurs, for the near and distant pasts. On the other hand, English is my public language, my language of the present, to resolve the immediate. It is the language my vocal cords use to argue, my language of reason and rational explanations, for professional prose and precise clarity, and for active offense—I can easily curse out and send anyone to hell in English; in Spanish it would take a lot. English is my otherness, my language for raising my voice and making myself heard, my language of the here and now. Yet, the moment I open my mouth and say something in English, it becomes clear that I am a "foreigner," that English is not my mother tongue. When I speak Spanish, my interlocutors can rarely deduce that I am Dominican, and when I am in the Dominican Republic, despite the fact that I immediately acquire my Dominican diction, my vocabulary betrays me (both the one I use, which shows certain traits of archaism, and lacks the current expressions I am not familiar with), and again stirs some doubt about the authenticity of my Dominicanness. This is precisely what Rumbaut points to when he says that Generation 1.5 ends up being marginalized in both the old and new worlds.

This "foreign" or "marginal" stamp leads to the questioning of origin as a determinant of identity, and in this dichotomy the idea of "home" (in all its connotations) creates a bridge between my relationships with the world and the world's relationship with me. I suppose I live bifurcated and on that bridge. Where is my home? Many of us have already asked ourselves this same question. As Isabelle de Courtivron (Professor of French Studies at MIT) wrote in her essay "Memories of a Bilingual Daughter":

> It's late August in Paris and I should be used to it by now. I am taking the plane tomorrow. "How wonderful that you are coming home!" my Boston friends tell me. "How sad that you are leaving home!" my Paris friends echo. Am I returning home or leaving home? After all this time I still don't know. Probably a bit of both (De Courtivron, 2003, 157).

I too have frequently faced a similar situation when making my journal entries. For example: when I return from a trip to another country or when I return to the Dominican Republic, when I am again seated at my work table, just as I get ready to write in my diary, at that precise moment of documenting the date, time, place, what do I write?: "At home"? "Back home"? What arises and surrounds me at those moments is the question, not the answer: Where or what is my home? Is it the one I live in and pay for, or is it the one I left behind, the one I would leave each morning for school in a khaki uniform? Is it the house that my daughter knows as hers? I think I haven't been able to fully answer that question. And how have I resolved it? Almost unconsciously, I began to write "At home" in quotes, as if that concept or this place were foreign, or belonged elsewhere.

§§§

IDENTITY

When it comes to the world's relationships with me, I am faced with the questioning of my identity. It is as if one becomes a foreigner in both countries. And, as I have mentioned before, in the United States as soon as I open my mouth many people ask me (and with good intent in most cases) where I am from. That happened to me frequently when I lived in Albuquerque, New Mexico, because there I could be physically identified as Latino or Hispanic, but when I spoke (both in Spanish and English) it became clear that I was not from there, leading to this questioning about my identity. In the Dominican Republic, I remember once I was on Las Salinas de Baní beach during one of those "homeward" trips, and a little boy approached me and the first thing he said was: "Look, an American!" I felt almost inexplicably offended—more than offended, I felt hurt, not because he called me "American" (I was born in the Americas, in the First City of America), but because that implied that he perceived me as a foreigner, a stranger. In her essay "The Mask and the Pen," Nancy Huston presents an interesting analogy in which she proposes that living in a foreign country and speaking a foreign language is like wearing a mask, and after years of wearing that mask, something happens to the face behind the mask. Huston wrote:

> You go "home" and people can't believe their ears. *What?* You call that your *mother tongue*? Have you seen the state it's in? I don't believe it! *You got an accent!* You keep slipping French words into your speech! It's ridiculous! Stop putting on airs! ... Come on, talk normally! How dare you make mistakes? (Huston 2003, 61)

I know that it's not only language that tends to rust; there is also a lot of vocabulary for which one has no equivalent in the linguistic repertoire—things one has learned in the new language and for which we simply have no frame of reference, nor can one speak or give an opinion intelligently in the other language. I admit that it is not pleasant at all to find yourself in such a situation. It has happened to me both in the United States and in the Dominican Republic. For example, a few years ago in my hometown, in an interview for the local television station when they asked me about my work in the United States, I fumbled. I work in a Department of Safety and Security, and it turns out that both English words (safety and security) have different connotations, and these words I learned/acquired in English. In Spanish, we have a single word for both things (seguridad), making the double name redundant in Spanish. I never learned them in a professional context, and although the closest would have been "Seguridad y Protección," that definition only occurred to me after I faltered, trying to avoid saying "Departamento de Seguridad y Seguridad." At that moment, facing the cameras, I found myself at a loss for words and had to resort to using other words to explain my daily work.

It goes without saying that staying afloat in both languages and cultures is not an easy task. In the film *Selena*, about the life of the tejano singer, there is an important scene when she is invited to perform for the first time in México. Her father, worried that the press would criticize Selena's gringa Spanish, tells her: "Anglos jump all over you if you don't speak English perfectly, and Mexicans jump all over you if you don't speak Spanish perfectly. We got to be twice as perfect. Nobody knows how tough it is to be Mexican American." And therein lies the greatest challenge: you have to be more American than the Americans, and (in my case) you have to be more Dominican than the Dominicans.

CONCLUSION

Today, living in this transtierro, we are usually free—barring pandemics, changing migration policies, and other unforeseen circumstances—to come and go from our current and previous "home countries" and thus continue to strengthen our roots here and there. This is true even in the case of Cubans, for whom the transtierro has been the inevitable result of a long-term exile (long enough to plant roots and develop alliances with the host country). And today it is the children of the exiles, or those who arrived at a very young age, who have begun to travel back to Cuba to meet relatives, foster friendships and amorous attachments, etc. Inevitably, there will continue to be changes in relations between Cuba and the United States, which will open doors and bridges to reestablish ties. And once those bridges are established and those migratory obstacles removed, the Cuban transtierro will take hold, just like with Dominicans and Puerto Ricans in the past. And there will be those who will surely want to go back to Cuba for good, and likely some actually will, the majority will return to the United States, since, as I pointed out at the beginning, "the host country has its own attractions, its own charms and certain advantages that the country of origin does not offer." With transtierro, we are all encompassed in common circumstances in relation to our homelands: almost without realizing it, the idea of permanently returning (or retiring) becomes a difficult proposition; there are more cases of people who have gone back and forth than those who stayed permanently. In many practical senses, both legal and emotional, we can appreciate that our home country is no longer the same: it is different, it has changed, and we too are no longer the same: we have changed.

Here and now, for many of us the idea of "going home," in its practical and pragmatic sense, is a crossroads, almost a paradox: in a moment we can be at home in the Dominican Republic (where we grew up) and the next day we can be at home in the United States (where our children grow up). Hence, transtierro is that condition that situates us on that bridge connecting our realities and identities and our cultural and linguistic bifurcation in both directions.

To conclude, I will once again quote Isabelle de Courtivron's essay: "When asked if she felt European or American, the publisher Helen Wolf replied with an Austrian saying: 'I am someone with two exiles and no country'" (De Courtivron, 2003, 164). Those of us who live on the transtierro bridge can repeat this verbatim, because we end up being exiled (in the sense of nearly becoming foreigners) in two countries and we live as entities bifurcated between two languages, two cultures, two systems, two (hi)stories. We can repeat it, because every day we must survive and emerge as individuals, individuals with our own stories: bilingual, bicultural, bifurcated, permeable, here and there, and with a conjoined identity in the condition of TRANSTIERRO.

AFTERWORD

On August 19, 2025, Paul Theroux, prolific author on travel and world-renowned for his novel *The Mosquito Coast* (1981) met with students at Dartmouth College and urged them to travel "with languages," that is, that they travel and learn languages even the least known. Words matter, and the repeated search for ways to define the complex process of moving and migrating testifies to the need of continuing to explore the challenges of being elsewhere.

We also need ways to define the condition of being elsewhere and Keiselim (Keysi) Montás adds to the current debate on migration by giving us a new term "transtierro" / "transtierra" / "transtierr*" focusing on bilingualism and biculturalism. Today the multiplication of languages surrounding migration challenges the possibility of remaining within boundaries. The linear migrations of a century ago are now marked by repeated migrations between countries and languages. Keysi is particularly interested in the creativity that is engendered by and within migration. He is a poet himself whose expressive poetic language is Spanish while his daily life for decades has been in English. When I was writing about contemporary migrations and the writers who spoke of their journeys, I had the opportunity to talk directly with many authors, I realized that the authors' moves between places and languages was grounded on a pre-existing multilingualism to which migration added additional layers. Keysi speaks about the obsolescence of the very language he employs in his poetry: writing from afar utilizes a language that has become something different from what is currently used in the Dominican Republic, from the very outset, different, from the very beginning from the language of daily exchanges. We exist in different codes and for Keysi, as for many Italian writers who came from elsewhere and moved to another elsewhere, that new code is often English.

The creativity that emerges from words in movement is often writing that speaks in one language but at the same time dialogues with all the idioms of migration, defining the complex relationship with being other while having a life in an elsewhere. The accents that define us (and I have one) symbolize an accented way of living the everyday. In talking about his experience Keysi states that he speaks with an accent, but he doesn't think with an accent. I would argue that in moving away from the familiar context in which we grew up, we inevitably think with an accent. We turn any familiar local into the unfamiliar and position ourselves as observers who turn the familiar into the unfamiliar for ourselves and for the people with whom we come in contact. As Keysi states, he is considered neither an American in the US, nor a Dominican in the Dominican Republic. Migrants have the ability to turn the *heimlich* into the *unheimlich*, as Freud would say, as our moving has taught us to look at everyday life through different interpretative lenses that impact the way we translate the present. Indeed, this is the case even for those who define themselves as "native" speakers. Those of us who come from elsewhere hold up mirrors to people who think a country belongs to them and offer "accented" reflections of the context, culture, and language. Those reflections ask the "natives" to see what is familiar for them through the unfamiliarity that we bring to it. Migrants do not come from a somewhere; they inhabit a repeated elsewhere that changes and becomes more "accented" through repeated migrations. This accent is a precious thing: it uncovers the unfamiliar in the familiar and vice versa, it challenges traditions, the status quo, and engenders cultural anxieties necessary to question what is considered monocultural and monolingual.

The autobiographical plays an important role in narrating the accent, as Keysi highlights in chapter four of this book. As a genre that borrows from other genres, autobiography makes the public personal and places the self at the center of narratives that look the public sphere directly in the eye (if it had one) and talks back, in this case, to the ways in which otherness and accented identities are talked about in the politics of everyday life.

Being a migrant means living between past and future in a present that creates real and imaginary connections with what is left behind and what one envisions the future will be. The present can become, therefore, a space of creativity and the transtierro, Keysi Montás proposes, asks for a space to speak in order to narrate the multiple migrant identities in destination countries. Destination countries need the narratives of alterity in order to understand their own present, future and their present living relationship with that alterity.

Such narratives are fundamental in understanding the transformation of space and place in destination countries. In his book *Space and Place: The Perspective of Experience* (1977), the geographer Yi-Fu Tuan describes the difference between place and space: place is what entraps a person, space is what a person dreams of and on which one can exercise agency. For many migrants the destination country becomes a place where it is impossible to develop that kind of affective relationship. In order to transform the location of migration into a space and create forms of belonging to it, one needs to have the chance to braid identities and languages together. That can be performed by transterrados who demand that their lives be a constitutive part of a national identity narrative.

Immigration to Transtierro is a powerful text that speaks to us about how to create connections between different subjective realities and contributes significantly to the study of belonging to a people on the move, a reality that today is becoming the norm rather than the exception.

GRAZIELLA PARATI
Paul D. Paganucci Professor of Italian Literature and Language
Dartmouth College

NOTES

1. According to the definition of the Dictionary of the Virtual Library of the Center for Research on Latin America and the Caribbean at the National Autonomous University of Mexico, "'transterrado' is explained as the adaptation of a continuation with Spanish from Spain by the participation of Spanish in Mexico. It is the endearing idea, for every empatriated person, of having two homelands." Source:
http://www.Cialc.unam.mx/pensamientoycultura/biblioteca%20virtual/dictionary/transterrados.htm and https://www.jornada.com.mx/2011/07/09/politica/008n1pol

2. This book focuses on "legal" migrants; but it is very clear that the heartbreaking experience of emigration does not require visas nor passports.

3. Adolfo Sánchez Vázquez was born in Algeciras in 1915, in, and spent his childhood in Málaga. In his youth he was active in the Unified Socialist Youth. After studying Philosophy at the University of Madrid, he emigrated to Mexico in 1939, along with other intellectuals, scientists, and artists, after the fall of the Second Spanish Republic during the Civil War. He obtained a Ph.D. in Philosophy from the National Autonomous University of Mexico, where he taught and was later appointed Professor Emeritus. He was president of the Philosophical Association of Mexico and a member of the Science Advisory Council of the Presidency of Mexico. He died in 2011, in Mexico City. Source: Wikipedia.
Matesanz, José Antonio. 2009. "De desterrado a transterrado: el exilio en Adolfo Sánchez Vázquez". Vida y obra : homenaje a Adolfo Sánchez Vázquez. Ambrosio Velasco Gómez, coor-dinador México: UNAM, Facultad de Filosofía y Letras. pp. 81-90.

Gaos, José. "¿Filosofía 'americana'?". *Cuadernos de Cultura Latinoamericana* 32 (1979) [Translation: Erin Goodman].

4. Again, not so much so in recent times, given the reputational damage done by the 2016-2020 years and the anti-immigrant sentiments and hatred it unleashed, and the multiple and repeated terrorist and hate crimes committed and directly inspired, encouraged and condoned by that administration, its apologists and the many elected public officials who continued to hold office and continued to spew their anti-immigrant and hate rhetoric. All this has been amplified by a the second (current 2025 and on) term of the same administration, which has moved from rhetoric to active and hostile persecution of immigrants. Again, it is of paramount importance to note and call attention to the terror and persecution unleashed against immigrants today, the consequences of which will have long lasting and devastating effects.

5. I can't but think of that kind of discourse being shouted at a crowd from the downward escalator the moment a certain shameful stain announced its presidential ambitions. But, there is also a familiar precedent to this linguistic reference in the Dominican historical context, which has to do with the presence of Haitian immigrants in the Dominican Republic. The term "perejil" (parsley) is a shameful application of the imposition of borders on geographies and bodies, by identifying "language as a bastion against foreign contamination" and was the pretext for the 1937 massacre. Today in the Dominican Republic, the "application of borders and limits, imposing them on geographies and on bodies, on flags and on anthems" is our daily bread, and there is an imminent danger that without prompt and conscientious intervention, genocide could break out yet again.

6. There is no doubt that the technological advances of the last forty years represent the most powerful phenomenon in the history of human development. In all the thousands or millions of years of human existence on the face of the earth, never before has such a gigantic advance been achieved in such a short time. Let's put the following in perspective: the first cellular phone call was made in April 1973, and the first cell phone hit the market in

1984; the device weighed 14 ounces and cost four thousand dollars. Although it seems incredible, the first program to access the Internet (that is, the World Wide Web, through a browser), was written in 1990; before then there was no public access to the Internet. Can anyone imagine today's world without cell phones or the Internet?

7.   According to data from the Puerto Rican Endowment for the Humanities, the average number of Puerto Ricans who emigrated to the United States annually in the 1930s was 1,800. This increased to 4,600 from 1941 to 1945; to 31,000 from 1946 to 1950; to 45,000 from 1951-1960. In fact, 1953 was the year with the highest emigration, amounting to 75,000 Puerto Ricans. Between the 1960s and 1970s, it dropped to 16,500. Better job opportunities on the island and the decrease in job supply in the United States explain the reduction. In fact, due to the massive reduction in employment, Puerto Ricans began to disperse, moving from New York to other states and regions of the country.
Cited in: "Diáspora puertorriqueña: ciclos migratorios y comu-nidades a distancia": Grupo Editorial EPRL, 28 de enero de 2010. Enciclopedia de Puerto Rico, Fundación Puertorriqueña de las Humanidades:
https://enciclopediapr.org/?
s=Di%C3%A1spora+puertorrique%C3%B1a%3A+ciclos+migratorios+y+comu
nidades+a+distancia

8.   https://www.pbs.org/wgbh/americanexperience/features/castro-cuban-exiles-america/

9.   http://jacketmagazine.com/35/iv-kozer-ivb-mansito.shtml

10.   Madeline Millán, a Puerto Rican writer living in New York City, has published four books, including *Leche/Milk* (Puerto Rico National Poetry Award, 2009) and *365 esquinas*. She teaches at FIT/CUNY. Source: REPEAT-ING ISLANDS News and commentary on Caribbean culture, literature, and the arts: https://repeatingislands.com/2016/03/19/echo-of-voices-bilingual-poetry-readings-at-cornelia-street-cafe/

11. http://lookingazul.blogspot.com/2013/02/normal-0-false-false-false-en-us-ja-x.html?q=Madeline

12. The "1.5 Generation" comprises individuals who, having been born abroad (Cuba), are raised, educated and come of age in the United States. For this group, the first generation is represented by the parents, who are fully of the "old" world, and the second generation is made up of the children born in the United States and fully integrated into the "new" world. Between these two generations are those that make up the "1.5 generation." *Life on the Hyphen*, Gustavo Pérez Firmat, 1994 (4-5).

BIBLIOGRAPHY

TO: **Territories of Migration**

Ambrosini, Maurizio. *Sociologia delle migrazioni (Sociology of Migrations).* Il Mulino, 2005.

Appadurai, Arjun. *Modernity at Large: Cultural Dimensions of Globalization.* University of Minnesota Press, 1996.

Ariolfo, Rosana. "Comida, lengua e identidad en el paisaje lingüístico (Food, Language and Identity in the Linguistic Landscape)." *Orillas Rivista d'Ispanistica,* no. 8, 2019, pp. 629–52.

Ariolfo, Rosana, and Laura Mariottini. *Lengua española para traducir e interpretar* (LETI) *(Spanish Language for Translation and Interpretation -SLTI).* Clueb, 2021.

—. "El español en el paisaje lingüístico italiano. Contexto, metodología y análisis de datos (Spanish in the Italian Linguistic Landscape: Context, Methodology, and Data Analysis)." *Paisaje lingüístico. Cambio, intercambio y mé-todos (Linguistic Landscape: Change, Exchange, and Me-thods),* edited by Mercedes De la Torre García and Francisco Molina Díaz, Peter Lang, 2022, pp. 13–40.

Ariolfo, Rosana, and Laura Mariottini, editors. "Paisajes lingüísticos de la migración. Contextos mediáticos, urba-nos y formativos (Linguistic Landscapes of Migra-tion. Media, Urban, and Formative Contexts)." *Lingue e Linguaggi,* no. 25, 2018.

Bagna, Carla, and Monica Barni. "Per una mappatura dei repertori linguistici urbani: nuovi strumenti e metodologie (Toward a Mapping of Urban Linguistic Reper-toires: New Tools and Methodologies)." *La città e le sue lingue. Repertori linguistici urbani (The City and Its Languages. Urban Linguistic Repertoires),* edited by Nicola De Blasi and Carla Marcato, Liguori, 2006, pp. 1–43.

Bajini, Irina, et al., editors. *Words for Eating: Discourses and Cultures of Food.*

LED, 2017. (Referenced in Calvi 2017)

Barnes, John Arundel. "Class and Committees in a Norwegian Island Parish." *Human Relations*, vol. 7, no. 1, 1954, pp. 39–58.

Berruto, Gaetano. "Sul significato della dialettologia percettiva per la linguistica e la sociolinguistica (On the Significance of Perceptual Dialectology for Linguistics and Socio-linguistics)." *Che cosa ne pensa oggi Chiaffredo Roux? Percorsi della dialettologia percezionale all'alba del nuovo millennio (What Does Chiaffredo Roux Think Today? Paths of Perceptual Dialectology at the Dawn of the New Millennium)*, edited by Monica Cini and Riccardo, Edizioni dell'Orso, 2002, pp. 341–60.

Bhabha, Homi K. *The Location of Culture*. 2nd ed., Routledge, 1994.

Calvi, Maria Vittoria. "Lingua, Memoria E Identità Nei Racconti Dei Migranti Ispanoamericani (Language, Memory, and Identity in the Stories of Hispanic American Migrants)." *Altre Modernità*, numero speciale, 2014, pp. 124–39.

—. "Food and Identity in the Milanese Linguistic Landscape." *Words for Eating: Discourses and Cultures of Food*, edited by Irina Bajini et al., LED, 2017, pp. 215–37.

—. "Hispanic Linguistic Landscapes: Panorama of Studies and New Perspectives." *Panorámica de estudios Lingüísticos*, no. 17, University of Valencia, 2018.

—. "Prácticas Transnacionales e Integración en el Paisaje Lingüístico de Milán." *Lengua y Migración / Language and Migration*, vol. 12, no. Extra 1, 2020, pp. 203–34.

Calvi, Maria Vittoria, Irina Bajini, and Marta Bonomi. "Migrant Languages and New Landscapes." *Altre Modernità*, no. 16, University of Milan, 2016.

De Fina, Anna, Deborah Schiffrin, and Michael Bamberg, editors. *Discourse and Identity*. Cambridge University Press, 2006.

Foner, Nancy. *American Arrivals: Anthropology Engages the New Immigration*. School of American Research Press, 2003.

García, Ofelia, and Li Wei. *Translanguaging: Language, Bilin-gualism, and Education*. Palgrave Macmillan, 2014.

Krefeld, Thórhallur. "For a Linguistics of Lived Space." *Lived Space and Linguistic Dynamics: Southern Varieties in Italy and in Situations of Extraterritoriality*, edited by Thórhallur Krefeld, Peter Lang, 2002, pp. 11–24.

Landry, Rodrigue, and Richard Y. Bourhis. "Linguistic Landscape and Ethnolinguistic Vitality." *Journal of Language and Social Psychology*, vol. 16, 1997, pp. 23–49.

Lobera Serrano, Fernando. "Being in Space." *Verbal and Nonverbal Languages: The Body in Spanish and Italian Language, Literature, and Culture,* edited by Francesca Liberatori and Maria Cristina Desiderio, Pioda Editore, 2010, pp. 53–61.

Mariottini, Laura. "On Linguistic-Discursive Identity: Theoretical Exercises for the Study of Latin American Migration in Italy." *Community Mediation: A Possible Experience,* edited by Demetrio De Luise and M. Morelli, Libellula Edizioni, 2012, pp. 117–39.

—. "Linguistic Policies and Latin American Migration in Rome: Monolingualism and Multilingualism in the Communicative Signs of the Public Space." *Political Languages: More Than Words,* edited by Felice De Cesare and Michela A. Giovannini, UniorPress, 2019, pp. 85–113.

—. "Urban Narratives: From Linguistic Signs to Social Practices of Integration." *The Reception of Migrants,* edited by Tiziana Grassi, One Group Edizioni, 2019, pp. 627–34.

—. "Linguistic Landscape and Frames: Spanish in Rome." *Orillas: Magazine of Hispanic Studies,* vol. 12, 2023, pp. 703–25.

Mariottini, Laura, and Francesca Orletti, editors. *Language, Interaction, Mediation: Latin American Migration to Italy.* Italian Studies in Theoretical and Applied Linguistics, Year XLII, vol. 3, 2013.

Mariottini, Laura, and Anna Oricchio. "Landscapes and Language Rome: Departure of a Geolocalized Platform as a Tool for the Study of the Linguistic Understanding of Migrant Spanish in Rome." *Cuadernos AISPI,* vol. 18, no. 2, 2021, pp. 257–80.

Oricchio, Anna. "Paisaje Lingüístico de la Migración Hispanoamericano en Roma: Signs and Perceptions." *Advances in the Studies of Hispánica Lingüística: Theoretical and Applied Perspectives Among Language and Society,* 2024, pp. 414–51.

—. "Identity, Visibility, and Territory: Practices of Reterritorialization of the Hispanic American Migrant Community in Rome." *Migrantes, XXXIII Immigration Report 2024,* 2024, pp. 62–72.

—. "Language, Football, and Hispanic American Migration: (Re)constructions of Identity Through AS Roma." *Language and Migration,* vol. 2, no. 18, 2025, [in press].

Riccio, Bianca. *Anthropology and Migration*. CISU University Information and Press Center, 2014, p. 309.

Schiller, Nina Glick, Linda Basch, and Cristina Blanc-Szanton. "Trans-nationalism: A New Analytic Framework for Understanding Migration." *Annals of the New York Academy of Sciences*, vol. 645, 1992, pp. 1–24.

Suárez-Orozco, Marcelo M. "Right Moves? Immigration, Globalization, Utopia, and Dystopia." *American Arrivals: Anthropology Engages the New Immigration*, edited by Nancy Foner, School of American Research Press, 2003, pp. 45–74.

Tani, Isao. "Linguistic Landscape and Atmosphere: Some Methodological Reflections." *Lingue e Linguaggi*, no. 25, 2018, pp. 107–23.

Uberti-Bona, Maria. "Examples of Heteroglossia in the Milanese Linguistic Landscape." *Lingue Cultura Mediazioni / Languages Cultures Mediation*, vol. 3, no. 1, 2016, pp. 151–66.

—. "The Study of the Linguistic Landscape in Milan: An Ethnographic and Spatial Perspective." *Lingue e Linguaggi*, no. 25, 2018, pp. 173–96.

Vertovec, Steven. "Super-diversity and Its Implications." *Ethnic and Racial Studies*, vol. 30, no. 6, 2007, pp. 1024–54.

—. *Transnationalism. Routledge*, 2009.

Wandl, Alexander. "Territories-in-Between: A Crosscase Comparison of Dispersed Urban Development in Europe." *A+BE | Architecture and the Built Environment*, vol. 10, no. 02, 2019, pp. 1–392.

TO: **Immigration to Transtierro**

Agulló, Juan. "Españoles en el exterior: ciudadanía con espinas." *El País*, 19 Feb. 2011,
elpais.com/diario/2011/02/19/opinion/1298070005_850215.html.

Blanco, Richard. Lecture on poetry at Dartmouth College, Oct. 2013.

Buffington, Sean T. "Dominican Americans." *Countries and Their Cultures*, www.everyculture.com/multi/Bu-Dr/Dominican-Americans.html.

Diccionario de la Biblioteca Virtual del Centro de Investigaciones sobre América Latina y el Caribe (CIALC), Universidad Nacional Autónoma de

México,
www.cialc.unam.mx/pensamientoycultura/biblioteca%20virtual/
diccionario/transterrados.htm.

Diccionario Etimológico Castellano en Línea (Diccionario Virtual de Etimología),
etimologias.dechile.net.

*Dictionary of the Royal Academy of the Spanish Language (Diccionario de la lengua
española, Real Academia Española—RAE)*, 22nd ed., dle.rae.es/?
w=diccionario.

De Courtivron, Isabelle, editor and contributor. *Lives in Translation: Bilingual
Writers on Identity and Creativity*. New York: Palgrave Macmillan,
2003.

Dorfman, Ariel. "The Wandering Bigamist of Language." *Lives in Translation:
Bilingual Writers on Identity and Creativity*, edited by Isabelle de
Courtivron, Palgrave Macmillan, 2003, pp. 29–37.

Enciclopedia de Puerto Rico, Fundación Puertorriqueña de las Humanidades,
www.enciclopediapr.org.

Espaillat, Rhina P. *Where Horizons Go: Poems*. Truman State University Press,
1998.

Flores, Juan. "Puerto Rican Literature in the United States: Stages and
Perspectives." *Recovering the U.S. Hispanic Literary Heritage*, vol. 1,
Arte Público Press, 1993.

Gutiérrez, Franklin. *Voces de Ultramar: Literatura Dominicana de la diáspora*.
Santo Domingo: Dirección General de la Feria del Libro, 2005.

Huston, Nancy. "The Mask and the Pen." *Lives in Translation: Bilingual
Writers on Identity and Creativity*, edited by Isabelle de Courtivron,
Palgrave Macmillan, 2003, pp. 55–67.

Jiménez, Arturo. "El exilio, doloroso y desgarrador para Adolfo Sánchez
Vázquez." *La Jornada*, 11 July 2011, p. 8, www.jornada.com.mx/
2011/07/09/politica/008n1pol.

Lazo, Rodrigo. *Writing to Cuba: Filibustering and Cuban Exiles in the United
States*. Chapel Hill: University of North Carolina Press, 2005.

Mansito, Nicolás, III. "In Favor of Babel: José Kozer in Conversation with
Nicolás Mansito III." *Jacket Magazine*, 28 Dec. 2007,
jacketmagazine.com/35/iv-kozer-ivb-mansito.shtml.

PBS. "Cuban Exiles in America." *The American Experience*, www.pbs.org/

wgbh/americanexperience/features/castro-cuban-exiles-america/.

Pérez Firmat, Gustavo. *Life on the Hyphen: The Cuban-American Way*. Austin: University of Texas Press, 1994.

Repeating Islands: News and Commentary on Caribbean Culture, Literature, and the Arts. repeatingislands.com/2016/03/19/echo-of-voices-bilingual-poetry-readings-at-cornelia-street-cafe/.

Rumbaut, Rubén G. "The Americans: Latin American and Caribbean Peoples in the United States." Americas: New Interpretive Essays, 1992, p. 288.

"The Agony of Exile: A Study of the Migration and Adaptation of Indo-chinese Refugee Adults and Children." Refugee Children: Theory, Research, and Services, edited by Fre-derick L. Ahearn Jr. and Jean L. Athey, Johns Hopkins University Press, 1991, p. 61.

Selena. Directed by Gregory Nava, Warner Bros., 1997.

Stolowicz, Beatriz. "Asilo y exilio: indicios de una ruptura." La Ventana, 12 July 2011, laventana.casa.cult.cu/.

Torres-Saillant, Silvio. "Before the Diaspora: Early Dominican Literature in the United States." Recovering the U.S. Hispanic Literary Heritage, vol. 3, edited by Virginia Sánchez Korrol and María Herrera Sobek, Arte Público Press, 2000.

Vázquez, Lourdes. "Una sola pregunta." Looking Azul, Blogspot, 2013, lookingazul.blogspot.com/2013/02/normal-0-false-false-false cn-us-ja-x.html.

William, Luis. Dance Between Two Cultures: Latino Caribbean Literature Written in the United States. Vanderbilt Uni-versity Press, 1997.

INDEX